PUTTING IT ALL
ON PAPER

PUTTING IT ALL
ON PAPER

THE MEMOIRS OF

SHUPIER JONES

ASKJUSTSHUPIER

PUTTING IT ALL
ON PAPER

Published By: Shupier Jones

AskJustShupier, LLC Atlanta, Georgia

Copyright © Shupier Jones, 2017

All rights reserved. No part of this book may be reproduced, scanned, or distributed in any print or electronic form without permission. Please do not participate in or encourage piracy of copyrighted materials in violation of the author's rights. Purchase only authorized editions.

Library of Congress Cataloging in Publication Data

Putting It All On Paper

ISBN: 978-0-9988144-0-7

Printed in the United States of America

Book Arrangement by: Simms Books Publishing

Jeirnear Barr- Editor

Vernetta K. Williams, PhD; Chrysalis Consulting, LLC: Editor

James C. Lewis: Photographer

OneTwoThree Multimedia-Damon Upshaw /MisterSoul: Book cover

"For my daughters, who have given me love and strength through my trials and tribulations. I am driven to be the best version of me, being your first role model and example of a strong woman."

TABLE OF CONTENT

FOREWORD

ACKNOWLEDGEMENTS

INTRODUCTION

Chapter 1
TAKING OUT THE TRASH
1

Chapter 2
HOW IT ALL STARTED
7

Chapter 3
INNOCENCE IS NO LONGER PRESENT
33

Chapter 4
BROKEN INTO MANY PIECES
67

Chapter 5
THE CRUTCHES REMOVED FROM UNDER MY ARMS
91

Chapter 6
PRESSURE ISN'T ALWAYS BAD
127

Chapter 7
OBEDIENCE IS BETTER THAN SACFICE
141

ABOUT THE AUTHOR

And the LORD answered me, and said, Write the vision, and make it plain upon tables, that he may run that readeth it.
-Habakkuk 2

FOREWORD

Many know her as Shupier, but I know her as Ro. Everyone calls me Mo, so together we are Mo and Ro (corny but true). The moment I met her, we clicked, not in a superficial manner but on a spiritual level. Her aura is good. Shupier has great energy and is the type of person who can actually SEE you. For all of the most commonly used reasons, Shupier and I both didn't associate with a bunch of women when we first met. Fast forward five years, Shupier is still one of the few women I consider a friend.

We all have a story, right? We all have situations and circumstances that have occurred throughout our lives that shape and mold the type of person we are and the trajectory of our journey on this Earth. Some people choose to be a victim of their circumstances and never truly reach their full potential because of that decision. Some people take the hand they're dealt and play it as best they can. A small group of extremely purposed people not only turn their situation around, but they also share their testimony in a way that inspires and encourages others who may be going through similar trials. Shupier is THAT person. The strength and courage it takes to not only endure and persevere, but turn around and tell that story to the world is beyond admirable.

The story you are about to read may take you on an emotional roller coaster. As a matter of fact, it definitely will. You will experience empathy, sorrow, joy, anger and everything in between. Beyond those emotions is a message that is sure to alter your way of thinking, a word from someone not only touched by God but created to show you to yourself in a way that resonates through your soul. When Ro told me she finished this book, I was so happy! She came to me when she was thinking about writing it, and I remember telling her...just write. Even if it's a little a day, get your story out. Don't worry about chapters or any particular order...just write. And write she did. I could say so much more about this phenomenal woman and her story, but it's time for you to read it yourself. My prayer is this book gives you a glimpse into the type of person Shupier is and the depth of what she has to offer this world. Enjoy!

-Monique R. Simms

ACKNOWLEDGEMENTS

Putting it all on Paper was probably one of the hardest tasks I had to complete during my adult years. I had to write about moments that haunted me for years. You may probably agree when I say, "Bad experiences from your past are better off left behind." In fact, I believed in those exact words wholeheartedly until unresolved issues resurfaced. Like clockwork, feelings of resentment, loneliness, confusion, depression and vulnerability arose. I learned fast that unhealthy emotions provoke certain behaviors in relationships. For that reason, I'm grateful for my GOD sent friend Monique Rose. She helped me tap into something life changing, which has allowed me to help others with similar trials. I will never forget when she said, "Just start writing." Immediately, those empowering words were embedded in my heart; from there, I started writing my first book. I will forever be grateful that the Creator allowed us to cross paths.

Moving forward to thanking my beautiful daughters, Lazaria and Layoni Leggett, for being so amazing during the course of my new venture. I'm here to say, "it's not easy raising children." Parenting is my motivation to fulfill part of my purpose (being a mother). I've come a long way because I push myself for them. I am their first teacher who instructs them about this thing called life. Children aren't born ready-made; they are taught to become what they see. I know they're watching me on a daily basis. Eventually, I'll leave them with a legacy that hopefully inspires them for the generations to come. I want them both to fulfill their purpose, no matter what obstacles come their way.

Next, "You never get to goals you set on your own." God sends earthly angels (God sent people) to help you along your journey. Therefore, I have to especially thank the angels in my life: My Mother Rosa and Step-Father Curtis Kinsey, Father Edward Williams, Brother Travis Jones, Sister Kayla Williams, Nephews, Grandparents, Uncles and Aunts, Best friend Everlena Brummage, Cousin T'aunna Jones, Friends Shedonna Alexander, Pia Melinda, Lashain Blake, Shawnte Smith, Gloria Perry, Malon Fuller,

Cadro Jerry, Tracey Mclean, Caramita Brown, Clients, and all other Family and Friends for giving advice or providing a listening ear. Whether you know it or not, all of you have made a big impact in my life.

Last but not least, I have to especially thank the Creator for every good or bad moment. In all honesty, it made me a better woman. Also, I would like to thank the readers in advance for taking time out of your busy schedules to read my book. It took a lot of courage for me to finally open up to tell the world. It has been a therapeutic journey, which is why I feel anyone who reads my book is a part of my life now. And just maybe, I'll be a part of yours when this book helps to set you free when you put all your "Untold Stories" on paper.

INTRODUCTION

Before you start reading, I have to warn you that this is not the type of book that will change your life overnight or offer a step-by-step guide to paradise. I didn't change overnight, so I can't expect for you to either. I had to learn that solving life issues is not some frozen dinner you can place in the microwave to be cooked in minutes. I'm not the type of person who makes promises I can't keep, but I can assure you of one thing: I've become an open book. I became ameliorated mentally as I wrote *Putting It All On Paper*. I understood life better after jotting down all my hidden secrets in a notebook. Believe me, this book explains why.

Life is like a math problem to me. Yes, there are multiple ways to solving a math problem, but one wrong step will change the answer. It's similar to you trying to solve personal issues with an unclear mind. You're bound to make an irrational decision. The unique thing about this is the stories are different from one another. Although you may have walked with someone on the same path, it was just for a season. Eventually, you both resulted to a different outcome when comparing relatable journeys. That's when you hear the saying, "I been there and done that." It's true that some have experienced similar trials, yet their reaction was totally different.

My reason for writing this book is to encourage you to write down the chapters of your life you constantly create that stop you from fulfilling your divine purpose. For most of you, it takes years to actually talk about your past experiences that leave a negative indentation on your heart. You're fully aware of the mixed emotions that have you up and down. Also, you continue life unwilling to forgive from your heart. Then, you think this type of behavior is normal. You look like you have it all together on the outside, but you're walking around with misery on the inside. On top of that, you're the first to preach. And, you became the go-talk-to person (the counselor in your clique) to help solve others' problems when you haven't fixed your inner issues because you haven't practiced what you preach.

It's sad that the world offers temporary moments to make you feel better, but as soon you get some alone time, your brain quickly reminds you about what happened years ago, causing you to feel emotionally unstable from entertaining thoughts and adding new ones. I call that part-time JOY. Needless to say, you'll never be completely free until you face the very fear that's been rooted and grounded inside during your childhood years. Ask yourself, "How can I fully understand myself if I don't fully know me?" You can't. You're only going to assume you know when, in actuality, you don't have the slightest idea.

After years of being haunted by the skeletons in my closet, I decided to set myself free from bondage with the help of the good LORD. *Putting it All on Paper* became an outlet, and as simple as it sounds, just using a pen and paper allowed me to write every untold story that brought me hurtful memories.

Honestly, I was the type of person who didn't know how to verbally express myself. Writing helped me understand why I reacted the way I did towards certain situations and why I kept going through the same thing over and over. Sometimes, you're so quick to point the finger that you forget the three fingers pointing back at you.

Hopefully, this book will encourage you to write all your untold stories and be released from inner demons. Finally, I learned that the power of writing helps strengthen your faith and see your vision clearer. You finally learn how to fight in a war that was already designed for you to win.

"My closed lips allowed my past to haunt me, but a pen and paper freed me from bondage."

--Shupier Jones

1

TAKING OUT THE TRASH

What happens when you put all your experiences, thoughts and feelings on paper? Before you give an answer, let me tell you my philosophy to that question. I feel writing is your personal view of your life. You may feel it is an opportunity to express your feelings by releasing unspoken words on paper. However, I believe there is more to a pen and a piece of paper. I strongly believe your statements can bring forth change in others' lives, whether negative or positive.

Many times, I have read a message or quote that made an impression on my mind, which caused a change in my life. In some cases, a particular passage helped me find a solution to my problem. I learned that reading encouraging words will take you further in life than words with no purpose at all. Most of my inspirations came from the bible. Every now and then, I would read a quote from a magazine or book or write down words that came from a person's mouth. I made it my business to apply those specific words to my life and share them with others going through similar situations. In fact, those very words brought relief to my relatives and friends. Those same encouraging words enabled peace in some part of their daily routine, especially the ones on the verge of having a setback. I definitely can relate because I experienced stumbling blocks during my childhood that troubled my adult years.

My life has been full of secrets that I swept under a rug, thinking they would never resurface. You would be surprised how your past comes to haunt you in your present and future. Usually, when your past visits, it's a possibility that you never faced your deepest experiences, feelings or thoughts, so these emotions come forth with no warning or greeting. They take over, consuming every part of your body and mind.

Sometimes, life is challenging when you are trying to balance your life and juggling past situations. I know from experience and had the audacity to carry negative past experiences for 23 years. Why would a living soul carry garbage for so long? I can answer that question with no problem because I dragged myself through that garbage. Although I took showers to remove the smell, deep down my mind had an addiction to misery of the past. Misery was the drug; my past was the dealer and I found the dealer through my thoughts.

I was that dealer's best customer! I made him rich by giving him power over my mind. I allowed him to dictate how I should feel on a day-to-day basis. I thought the remedy was to cover my face with makeup and dress like a supermodel to cover the buildup in my heart. There's a saying that says, "Looks can be deceiving." I would have been the perfect candidate to do a commercial on that statement. I made myself look all pretty on the outside, but inside, I was full of hurt and pain.

People would often say, "You're a beautiful girl," or "You can have any guy you want." Honestly, my mind took me so far from believing that I was beautiful and anyone would ever truly love me. Instead of putting my thoughts and feelings on paper, I placed them under that rug and prayed they would just go away and never return. Those thoughts left, but, just when I grasped onto a little happiness, the urgency of my addiction arose. Once again, I felt powerless and alone with no one to rescue me.

With time, that feeling was about to change.

"The truth can catch up to a lie, but a lie will never catch up to the truth."

--Shupier Jones

2

HOW IT ALL STARTED

It was mid-1980 in Lake City, Florida.

My beautiful mother, Jean moved from a small, southern town to the big city of Miami, Florida. She was a southern girl with a little spice of city in her bones. She began her education in Miami at a two-year college, where she met and fell in love with a man. Leon was a tall, muscular man with even dark skin who spoke intelligently, as words flowed from his lips. His muscular build had many afraid of him because he was known for his martial arts skills.

In other words, *he would kick your ass in a heartbeat!*

In the course of their relationship, Leon cheated on my mother with other women. Their relationship was like a boat sailing in the middle of the ocean during a rain storm. Although the land was visible through my mother's sight, she knew the relationship was hopeless. She knew her survival on the boat relied on a cool summer breeze and her skin feeling the warmth of the sun peeking through sequenced clouds. She felt like the fewer the storms, the smoother the boat would sail. Once the boat made it to shore, Leon's cheating habits influenced my mother to lay eyes on another man. All her buildup directed her slowly towards Leon's roommate James.

James, a well-groomed man, believed in respecting women. His slim, athletic body and light caramel skin projected a very attractive man. He was very outgoing. James was the type of man that was loved by many and hated by few. His upbringing and mannerisms made people feel comfortable conversing with him. James' daily living represented order since he was military oriented. He was the complete opposite of Leon, who believed in having more than one woman at a time. Jean started a serious relationship with James after her so-called separation from Leon. James provided my mother with the comfort and security she needed. Although James' heart was pure, Jean saw the purity as a weakness, allowing her the opportunity to come in and out his life.

At the age of 22, Jean's struggle between two men did not take away the fact that her heart was with Leon. She was the rope in the game of tug of war. In the middle of a tug, she realized that she was going to play a real game of motherhood.

And I was her star player.

Facing two potential fathers placed Jean in an uncomfortable position during her time of pregnancy because she was forced to decide between Leon and James.

"Jean, if you walk out with Leon, then it's over between us two," James told her.

During that moment, Jean was so convinced that Leon was my birth father that she said, "James, this isn't your baby."

James replied, "Are you sure?"

"Yes," said Jean.

Walking out of James' life yet again, Jean got into a car with Leon and drove off. Without attempting to fight to keep Jean by his side, James knew only time would tell if he was the birth father. It was only a matter of time before Jean would end up back at James' apartment. Jean was a woman with a quick talk game who knew that James had a soft heart for her, so she waited about six months in her pregnancy to open the line of communication again. When Leon and she were on bad terms, Jean escaped to James' apartment for comfort. Jean didn't know Leon was on her trail; she also didn't know he knew she was visiting James from time-to-time.

As usual one day when she felt the need to visit James, Jean drove to his place after class, not knowing that Leon was in a friend's car camped in the front of the apartment. When Jean parked her car, she got out and walked up the stairs. Leon watched her go inside. His body movement changed as blood rushed to his brain. His veins became noticeable on the side of his forehead, the sweat from his fingertips smeared across the rubber on the top of the wheel; at that moment, Leon became more and more upset.

Jean didn't know that she was playing with fire. She loved going to James' place because she felt free and comfortable. When she entered, they both sat on the sofa while talking and watching the sports channel. After 20 minutes, Jean walked toward the kitchen to get something to drink.

After waiting in the car about 30 minutes, Leon couldn't resist any longer. He had waited long enough, so he got out of the car and took the stairs to the second floor (with thoughts of choking Jean crossing his mind).

Jean closed the refrigerator, took three steps, opened the cabinet and grabbed a glass cup. She heard a loud banging noise coming from the front door. It startled her so badly, and the first person she thought it could be was Leon. Instantly, she rambled to James, "I'm not here." Then, she ran into his bedroom to hide inside the closet on the left side of the room. Feeling confused, James rushed to the door, wondering who could be knocking. As he opened the door,

James was shocked to see Leon with a furious look on his face.

> James quickly asked, "What's up man? I haven't seen you in a while. What are you doing here?"

> Leon responded in an angry tone as he looked around for Jean, "Where is she? I seen her come in!"

Leon stormed past the living room into James' bedroom, looking under the bed and in the bathroom. James remained calm because he felt he had nothing to hide. Dramatically, Jean screamed from the top of her lungs when the closet door opened. Leon and Jean started fussing. She feared for her life when he snatched her by the right arm from out of the closet then pushed her on the bed. She kicked him with her right leg to get away, but before Jean could balance herself, Leon slammed her to the ground, then raised his left leg backwards to kick Jean in the stomach.

James distracted Leon by yelling loudly, "Man, she's pregnant! You going to hurt her and the baby." He intervened just in time by tackling

Leon on his left side; they started fighting in the bedroom. Jean got up and ran back into the living room to grab her belongings. She looked quickly one last time at them both before speed walking out the door with tears flowing, stomach pain, and bruises on her arms. She got in her 1982 blue Mercury Capri and quickly left them fighting.

Leon wasn't going to stop until revenge was served. James slammed Leon into the living room. When Leon got up, they wrestled out the door onto the second floor over to the bar rail. Leon had more of an advantage since James' back was against the bar rail and his body structure was no comparison to Leon's. James was very scared, so he did whatever he could to save his life. When Leon wrapped his hands around James' neck, James used both thumbs to poke Leon in the eyes until they started hurting. Then, Leon yelled like a little boy crying for his mommy. When he couldn't bear the pain any longer, he finally let James' neck loose. James hesitated for a quick second, eventually realizing he was free. Short of breath, he managed enough strength to run inside the apartment for his gun. He grabbed his phone to call the cops. With all the commotion, the neighbors peeked out their windows and doors. Everything happened so fast that when James went back outside, he saw Leon leaving in an unfamiliar black car. James showed Leon that he wasn't scared of him.

His neighbor walked over to him and asked, "Hey, Are you okay man?"

Breathing heavily, James answered, "Yeah, I'm okay man."

After that day, James wasn't too fond of Leon. The truth is James saved my life while I was in my mother's womb. Hearing this story later helped me to understand I have purpose on earth. My life was spared for a reason and that reason will soon be revealed.

Knock! Knock! Who's there? ... 9 months later!

I was born December 14, 1982, at Lake Shore Hospital. My mother went back to Lake City, Florida, to give birth to me. She was the oldest of 13 siblings, so her support system was with family. During this time, my mother had a three-year-old son under the care of my great-grandmother. It destroyed Jean mentally to see her only son being raised by another relative. As a result of her hurt, my mother challenged herself by creating goals that would better her financially. It gave her the sense of knowing her children were her number one priority. For that main reason, Jean made sure my brother knew that she was his main provider.

Meanwhile, Jean held me in her arms after my birth. She was positive this little chocolate baby was Leon's daughter. She felt most of my characteristics favored him. However, deep down, a part of her was unsure who could be my birth father.

After a healthy delivery, Jean stayed in her hometown for a short time then moved back to Miami into James' apartment. Somehow, she prompted him into letting me (the baby) and her move in with him.

Although James was clueless about being the father, he still greeted Jean with open arms. Since Jean was done with her two-year degree, she utilized her time wisely by working two jobs: a doctor's office by day and auto shop by night. Working those two jobs became very stressful for my mother. Many nights she came home exhausted. During her free time, all she did was sleep because working two jobs took most of her time. Needless to say, her mind was made up, so motherhood took a back seat to her disease called work-alcoholism-- nothing could stop Jean once her mind was made up.

Jean only lasted in James' apartment for about two years. James realized they were better off being friends than lovers; Jean overstayed her welcome with her aggressiveness, cheating habits and sneaky ways. Jean was always known for having a backup plan in case something happened. James had no idea that Jean applied for her own apartment for the both of us. When she mentioned to James that she was moving into her own place, they agreed on dividing the living room furniture so she would have something to start with. Even though the relationship ended, Jean remembered great qualities about James. He showed her how a man should provide and protect his family. She remembered those two qualities to help her choose the next man wisely, but Leon made those thoughts go out the window very quickly.

Jean's love triangle was like a child full of energy who can't be stopped from running around and getting into everything.

Facing the Truth

Seven years passed. During that time, my mother accomplished some of her goals. She became a homeowner by the time she turned 26. However, Jean's question regarding who was my birth father was still left unanswered. Who could be the father? Can you imagine how confusing that must have been for her? You may feel the thought of not knowing my biological father was a sad situation for Jean to go through as a single parent. Jean felt taking up most of the parenting would take away some of the aggravations between Leon and her. Meanwhile, Leon was ahead of his game. During his late twenties, he becomes a realtor, agent and made millions. For that very reason, my mother kept him on her radar. Jean loved getting that money. She liked the big house and the fancy cars. I remember going to visit him with my mother. A security guard always stopped us before entering the gated community. I didn't like going there because my mother would leave me downstairs watching television while Leon and she went upstairs.

As a child, I felt excited and confused at the same time because it was hard for me to solve this father mystery. I was six years old, so seeing Leon and James every blue moon had me confused on who to call father. In most cases, men would not play the father role in this situation. In spite of not knowing who could be my father, Leon and James made it their priority to provide me with love, protection and guidance when in their presence. There is nothing like receiving father support from two different men, but God only made one man to fulfill that position. Although my world should feel complete with some type of father structure, more clues still needed to be gathered to solve this mystery. Internally, I felt more incomplete than anything because a part of me yearned for a father and daughter bond. I wanted to feel connected to my birth father, but we all were insecure with our parts of this father and daughter relationship.

Leon, however, had another agenda. His controlling personality couldn't keep on living with the fact of not knowing if he really was my father. Jean made sure that he was aware of the possibility that I could be another man's child, but when Leon found out that the other potential father was James, he was furious! He wanted to hurt Jean in the worst way by taking me away from her. Leon knew taking me away would turn my mother's world upside down. So, he decided to hire a lawyer to get full custody of me. Since everything processed through the proper protocol, Jean received a letter stating that she must be present in family court. Leon was the detective in this unsolved father mystery. His patience reached its capacity and one twist of the door knob would set the truth free.

Overburdened with mixed emotions, Leon didn't care who would get hurt in this situation. His emotional thinking tangled his mind by convincing him into believing that he was my father. Leon was so convinced that he didn't need test results to clear up what he already felt he had an answer to. All his mind was set on was getting revenge against my mother. Leon's hurtful situation caused him to want to pull my mother's heart out with his bare hands so that she would feel his escalating pain. His hurt consumed every part of his body, but only the voice of a judge and written document would satisfy his evil desires or crush his entire plan.

The Day of Court

The final clue to this father mystery was a moment we all had been waiting for. My mother waited seven years for the solving of this case. The only way this case would close was with both of them standing before a judge.

The day of the court appointment was a beautiful Monday morning. Jean decided to dress me in a beautiful yellow flared dress. I wore white sandals and yellow and white hair bows around my two ponytails. Sitting down on the living room sofa, I watched my mother pace the floor back and forth making sure that she had all her important papers. I could tell that she was very nervous, but she knew it was time for the truth to be revealed. After we were completely dressed, Jean took me by the hand, and we walked out the house to her white Toyota Corolla she'd bought from James.

Sitting in the back seat of the car, I noticed the ride seemed a little longer than usual. My curiosity arose, and my eyes started gazing out the back window and saw big buildings that looked as if they were touching the sky. When the car came to a complete stop, my mother opened the car door on my side to let me out. She then grabbed my hand, and we walked across the street from the parking lot into a tall building. My mother went up to a counter; I looked around and saw the majority of everyone wearing business attire with briefcases and paperwork in their hands.

> The officer pointed in the direction, saying, "*Go down to the end of the hall, then make a right and the courtroom will be the first door on the left.*"

My mother said, *"Thank you, sir."*

When we entered the family court room, another officer directed us to the gallery in front of the judge's bench. It was very diverse with people sitting in the courtroom waiting for their cases to be called. Leon sat away from us on the left side of the courtroom looking over paperwork. We walked to the right side of the court room to the third row and sat next to a Caucasian couple. They introduced us to their beautiful grand-daughter Ashley. She was well-mannered with an imagination. She waited for her grandparent's permission for every movement she made. My mother gave me eye contact, letting me know it was alright to speak back because she taught me not to speak to strangers unless I was told to do so.

I looked at Ashley and said with a soft voice, "My name is Ronesha." I was a bit nervous in the beginning, but a short while later, our parents had no problem telling us to be quiet. Ashley and I made our time in the court room useful. Our extraordinary imaginations made us believe that we were little princesses having a tea party in a castle. For a moment, our world was peaceful and there wasn't a single worry present. But, every princess story has the evil villain. Our tea party was crashed by the evil witch, who snatched my paper tea cup out of my hand to have it as her own, which instantly snapped us out of fairy tale world and turned everything back to its original form. I then realized my mother wasn't the evil witch any more, but an upset mother who wanted her important documents out of our hands before we destroyed them.

> *"Ronesha, give me those documents. These papers aren't toys baby."* My mother whispered, but I knew she meant business.

I looked at my mother with a sad puppy look and put my head down because I was full of shame. Then, all of a sudden, the lawyer called out my mother's last name to report to the front table.

> *"Order, all rise,"* the Officer said during the entrance of the Judge.

Then, the Officer handed a folder to the Judge and told us that we may be seated. Jean had no idea that Leon wanted full custody of me until the Judge mentioned why she had a trial date. My mother's facial expression looked more hurt than anything. The Judge looked at both parents' living arrangements and decided the both could have joint custody after the results of a DNA test.

For a second, I heard the sound of my mother's heartbeat that sounded like a drummer playing drums during church services. I believe her heartbeat was a representation of relief escaping from agony. Years of sweeping her situation under the rug came to an end; it was now time for the dust to be swept from under the rug. At the end, the Judge reviewed the case and told Jean if the DNA test should have any other results that didn't pertain to this case; she would not have to return to court. In other words, if Leon turned out not to be the father, then my mother was withdrawn from the case.

"Court is now adjourned," said the Officer.

My mother stood up and grabbed all her belongings because we were leaving the courtroom. I could tell that my mother was very mad with Leon for wanting full custody of me. The edginess showed on Jean's face, and I could tell that she wasn't in a very good mood. Jean couldn't resist the uneasy feeling inside, so she walked over to Leon and looked at him with a serious look on her face. When she opened her mouth, it was like hearing a tiger's roar, an untamed wildcat who felt the need to protect her baby cub from a threat.

> *"You're an asshole! How dare you try to take my baby from me? All you think about is your damn self, you dirty bastard,"* Jean said.
>
> *Leon looked at Jean and smiled, letting her know that he intended to follow through with his plan. "She belongs with me Jean,"* he said.
>
> My mother said, *"Kiss my ass you fucker!"*

Suddenly, there was a big commotion between Leon and my mother; it made everyone in the court room stop what they were doing to look at them argue. Only the judge and the officer were able to stop them from disrupting the court room. Three officers came out of nowhere to escort them to the judge's stand for disorderly conduct.

"You both are adults acting like little children fighting over a piece of candy! If I hear another outburst like that, I will hold the both of you in contempt," the judge said firmly.

"I strongly recommend getting your acts together before you both spend a cold night in jail," he explained.

The judge dismissed Leon first, then informed my mother that it would take two weeks for the test results to come in the mail, so until then, she would just have to be patient. I saw a tear rolling down my mother's face as she turned around from the judge's stand. She scuffled with her papers and purse as she grabbed my hand. When she came back to her senses, my mother knew she had to behave accordingly to keep us from separating. Meanwhile, I glanced through the courtroom one last time looking for my new friend Ashley. When I made eye contact with her, I lifted my hand and waved goodbye, for that was the last I would see of her.

My little legs kept getting tangled as my mother and I stormed out of the Family Justice Center building. When we made it inside the car, Jean took her car keys out of her purse, inserted the key into the ignition, looked at me through her rearview mirror and started weeping as we drove out of the parking lot. During the ride, I witnessed a sensitive side of my mother because it wasn't that often that I saw her cry. I guess the thought of Leon having full custody of me devastated her. Although she was not all that good at expressing her feelings, I learned that day how valuable I was to Jean and knew it would take a couple of days until she returned to her normal self.

When the second week came, Jean checked the mailbox every day religiously. One day coming home from work, Jean rushed to her mailbox to see if she received the DNA results. She opened the mailbox and pulled all the mail out. As she scrambled through the mail, she came across a letter from the DNA lab. Jean opened the letter and started reading it slowly. You could see the tension in her chest and hear her heavy breathing; her sweaty palms began to saturate through the paper and her eyes stopped at the results.

As her eyes started to tear up, it was clear for once in her life that Jean was certain of one thing: Leon wasn't her child's father. A feeling of overwhelming relief left her body, freeing her from the burden of not knowing her child's father. Jean was so excited that if the Judge had been in front of her, she would have kissed him; instead, a scream came out of her lungs like lava coming from a volcano. I ran outside to see what was going on because the way she yelled, made me believe she was in danger. Her scream made such an impact in our development that the neighbors came outside their doors too. When reality struck her mind, Jean looked around the neighborhood and saw the neighbors and me staring directly at her.

Quickly, Jean said, "I'm okay, everyone! Just read some good news."

In the midst of this awkward moment, you could see the skin on Jean's forehead scrunching together from her eyebrows lifting up; her smirk transitioned her cheekbones upward, making her audience believe that she was unharmed. A few seconds later, she held up the letter and waved it from side-to-side at her curious neighbors. Afterwards, she walked towards me, placed one arm around my shoulder and pulled me close to her as we went inside the house. Now, you may be curious of what is next. Allow me to carry on...

> "I will get my innocence back even if I have to go through my past to get it."
>
> --Shupier Jones

3

INNOCENCE IS NO LONGER PRESENT

What is innocence? Innocence is defined as a lack of knowledge or understanding. But, is this true? Most people wouldn't make innocence a topic of discussion because it could be viewed in so many ways. I feel that the word gets over looked, pushed to the side and left untreated for many reasons. For instance, when I think of a child who died running from gunfire, an elderly man who had to be hospitalized from the beating of gang members, a college student who was raped on campus after a group study, or a drunk driver who killed a family in a car accident, I consider the presence and the loss of innocence.

I feel pain for those who became victims when their innocence was stolen by others who didn't treasure its meaning. In some cases, you may feel it's meaningless to some degree because at some point in your life, you've encountered your innocence being taken away and felt no need for it to return. Should an individual move forward believing that his or her innocence is no longer present? If your answer is yes, I believe you made the wrong decision. Unfortunately, millions of people live up to this sad belief.

Just imagine how many people blame themselves for innocent moments they've experienced being taken away--right before their very eyes. In fact, I conceived and nourished this very same act, carrying blame for lost innocence inside of me like a baby in a mother's womb. It wasn't until later in life that I learned the value of innocence and how easy your mind can manipulate you into believing you're the reason it can be taken away. For instance, when you allow a negative thought into your mind, it's no longer beneficial to your body because it becomes a dangerous war in your self-conscious. *Pause.* Re-read that last sentence; let it take you into thinking mode, so you're able to get the full effect of it. If you did, that's a good thing because the next experiences, thoughts and feelings I'm putting on paper will give you a better view on why I think the word innocence should no longer be treated like a step-child.

Face-to-Face Conversation

My mother waited a couple of days to tell James that he was my biological father. She called him to come over to the house one Saturday morning to relay the news face-to-face instead of telling him over the phone. She felt this important information should be told in person instead of over the phone. So, James agreed to meet with my mother after handling his other business.

When James pulled into our driveway, I looked out the window when I heard his truck door slam. I ran into my mother's room to let her know that her guy friend had just pulled up in front of the house. A few seconds later, the doorbell rang; my mother paused with a nervous look on her face as she walked out of the room to open the front door. Then, all of a sudden, she stopped in the middle of the hallway, looked into the mirror to fix her cleavage, lifted her right hand up to straighten her long black hair and turned, taking one last deep breath as she proceeded to the door.

My eyes opened wide and my heart started beating quickly because the father figure I had longed for was finally standing on our front porch. I was so nervous that I stood close behind my mother as she unlocked the door. The wider the door opened, the more I grabbed hold to my mother's silky white blouse. I was so close to her that you would have thought I turned into my mother's hip bone. Believe it or not, I was like her motion detector, catching on to her every move. When she finally opened the door, James saw the both of us scuffling over my mother's blouse.

In a discomforting voice, my mother said, "Come in James and have a seat. Please don't pay us any mind. She is just a little timid right now for some strange reason."

James had a shocking look on his face as he walked past us into the living room area. His look made me instantly stop holding on so tight to my mother's silky white blouse. In the middle of me detaching my hands from her blouse, my mother said to me,

"Go to your room and do not come out until you are told to young lady."

By the sound of her voice, I could tell that she was a little aggravated with me and needed a few minutes to calm down. I shouldn't have allowed shyness to confound me, but the inner child somehow freed herself. As weird as I felt, I closed my room door and turned on the television to watch some cartoons.

Two hours had gone by, and I arose from a nap. I knew it was later in the day because the afternoon cartoons were showing. After stretching and getting myself together, I wanted to know if James and my mother were still talking in the living room. So, I reached for the remote and turned the television off, but heard complete silence. I eased up quietly, cracked the door open and took a sneak peek, but no-one was around. I decided to walk into the living room without my mother's permission. I had to make sure I didn't mumble a word while roaming around the house because I didn't want to get caught being disobedient towards my mother's rules. After a few steps, I noticed there wasn't a visible soul in sight. I continued walking towards the kitchen, but there wasn't anyone there either. At this point, I started to panic; I felt like I was home alone.

Then, it hit me; I missed one part of the house my mother's bedroom. As I tiptoed down the hallway, the closer I got to the door, the more curious I became. Suddenly, thoughts rushed through my mind. I assumed my mother accidently left me home alone. Then, I thought of aliens taking my mother to another planet to do strange things to her. My thinking didn't stop with that; I went on to believe that the neighbor's brown pit-bull swallowed her whole body. It was clear that the only thing that would control my thinking was to open her bedroom door. When I reached to turn the door knob, my right hand began to shake a little. I was so scared that I felt fear racing freely through my body.

I started debating back and forth until I built up enough courage to turn the knob. When the door opened, it was pitch black only because my eyes were still closed. The look on my face showed that I was scared, so I stood in the doorway in complete silence waiting to hear the sound of my mother's voice. When I heard nothing, I peeked with my right eye and counted four bare feet at the edge of the bed, which caused my left eye to open. I looked around with both eyes and saw there weren't any aliens or a dog in my mother's room. However, I did see the both of them sound asleep in the bed with James lying naked on top of my mother. Immediately, my vivid imagination withered away like chaffs in the wind. I paused for a moment with every intention to turn around and head back into my room and act as if I didn't see anything.

At that moment, I thought of a time when I was watching a movie and saw two naked people about to have sex, but my mother covered my eyes, rescuing me from being exposed to sex at an early age. After briefly contemplating, reality resurfaced and I realized my mother could not be my hero because she was part of an experience that desensitized me to sex as a little girl. The thought of James and my mother having sexual intercourse left me with a despicable feeling.

It was an unforgettable moment that was hard to let go. It caused me to question myself over and over again, "Why was Mr. James lying naked on top of my mother?"

> Like a typical seven-year-old, I muttered, "Ewwwww! I just saw mommy lying naked with Mr. James."

I had a dumbfounded look on my face after that surprising encounter. A sense of urgency took over me, and all I wanted to do was head back into my room before my mother noticed me at the foot of her bed. It was hard for me to believe that I was able to shut the door since my fingertips barely grabbed the knob. At that point, I felt unsure how to accept what I had just witnessed. When I entered my room, I started mumbling to myself while pacing back and forth from the television to the bed. Afterwards, I fell backwards on top of my pink comforter that covered my bed and lay there with my arms on the back of my head as I stared at the ceiling. The more I stared at the ceiling, the more heaviness consumed me. I found myself entertaining thoughts I wasn't sure about. I guess I was more frustrated with the fact of not knowing the type of relationship James and my mother had going on. So, the race began with negativity in the lead and positive thoughts coming in last, which caused veins to pop out from the side of my temples. I gritted my teeth together, took a deep breath, then placed my pillow over my head to calm my thinking down. Moments later, their voices came through the walls into my bedroom, and I knew they were wide awake from the volume of their heavy chatting. Jean's charming personality somehow managed to get James behind closed doors. You could tell she enjoyed every moment of his company from her giggles and repeated questions. It was a while since I had heard excitement come from my mother's voice.

As I heard the sound of footsteps coming towards my door, I hurried up and closed my eyes and turned my back to face the door to fake like I was still asleep. The last thing I wanted my mother to know was me sneaking out of my room and walking in on James and her during their naked encounter. When I heard knocking at my door, I stayed in the same position until my mother opened my room door.

"Ronesha," she yelled.

"Wake up babe," my mother said.

I turned around, acting as if I just came out of a deep sleep. I looked at my mother as I rolled out of bed and followed her into the living room. James stood in the middle of the living room with a nervous look on his face. He tried smiling but this revelation made it a little hard for him to do. It made me feel awkward because we stood there speechless and looked clueless at the same time until my mother bent down in front of me with both of her knees touching the ground, grabbed me on the sides of my arms to pull me close and said,

"James is your birth father!"

After making her statement known, I bet you are wondering what my comeback was! It was more like body talk. If I could describe my reaction in any type of way, it would be like a plastic bottle of water placed in the freezer overnight. If a bottle of water is placed in the freezer overnight, you'll find the water to be difficult to drink because it became a frozen substance. Well, that's the perfect example of how I reacted to my mother's statement. I was like a frozen water bottle placed in the freezer. She had to shake me over and over again until I snapped out of my stiffness. My mother expected me to be more excited, but my reaction came across cold.

After eight years, I finally knew my birth father. Jean wanted me to greet James with open arms, but that day, I didn't. I just grinned and looked at him with innocent eyes as he hoped for a better response from me too. Since the atmosphere was weird, everyone stood in the same position until James patted his left leg with his hand while in an odd posture. I watched him as he inhaled through his nose and blew out his mouth before he said, "How are you?"

"*I'm fine,*" I responded in a very low tone.

Little did they know the thought of seeing them both naked skimmed cross my mind again.

That was one thought I didn't care too much about. The queasiness coming from my stomach made me want to vomit. I was feeling that everything was being rushed, so my body started doing its own thing. Truth is, I don't know what child in his or her right mind wants to see his or her parents reenact Adam and Eve's nakedness.

The very thing I didn't want was to be surprised after seeing them in the moment of their mating season. If I could have my way, I would have blinked them away with my eyes like a genie, then tried the meet and greet thing another day. I knew my brain needed more time to adjust and accept that James would be playing an important role in my life. Now that the truth had been revealed, he would no longer be referred to as Mr. James. Honestly, I think that was the part that scared me the most.

I called for help but no-one came...

Once I knew my biological father, you would've thought my life was a lot better with both parents present. Well, I hate to bust your bubble because it wasn't---not even close. James' absence and being withheld from the truth intervened in the middle of our family reunion because we lacked a father and daughter connection. Although I was his only child at the time, it was sad that he knew very little about me. I wanted an instant connection between the both of us, but the lack of time and lies didn't allow it. I have realized being misled for some time affected our chances of getting to know each other like we should. My mixed emotions caused me to have some restrictions during our bonding time. Since James made an effort, I felt my acceptance mattered to him and it was very important for me to be a part of his life, but absence became James' spokesperson. I realized our relationship would be a work in progress.

When you're involved in a situation like this, you ask yourself, "Where should I start? Should I keep moving forward in life without my biological father?" Honestly, I wrestled with these questions many times. Regardless of James not being present, I felt he should have known something about me---*for the sake of God, this man is my father.* I figured there should've been an instant connection between the two of us: some type of warmth, security or completeness should have prevailed. I assumed during that time that clarity should've made a grand entrance, but I only remembered confusion and remorse couldn't stand a chance against the lost times. I became a child who was flustered about why I had to wait so long to know the truth.

The bible says, "And you will know the truth, and the truth will set you free." (James 8:32, KJV.) Although the truth was revealed, I was far from feeling free. My mother seemed to be, but I was left feeling like a rope tied into many knots. I felt the need to become demanding and impatient rather than gradually letting the connection take its course. The truth about my birth father was withheld from me for seven years, which made it difficult for him to take away this empty void of disappointments. I partially blamed my mother because during those seven years she was blinded by who she thought was the man for her.

If I had to describe Leon's love for Jean, I would have to say it was like a robber breaking into a rich couple's home while they were having a romantic outing on their yacht. You would have thought a rich couple getting away for a romantic sailing would appear to be innocent; instead, their home was invaded.
Jean's assumption that she was doing the right thing caused her a life-threatening moment--- Leon's counterfeit love. Leon's manipulative character was one way he controlled how my mother perceived him. Even though the sky was clear to sail on the yacht (life), it crippled her mind. From the outside looking in, you thought her home (love) was secured.
When you imagine Leon being the robber, it's sad to know he was the only one who knew the time and hour to rob my mother's home (love). He watched the neighborhood frequently just to monitor her whereabouts, ensuring that nothing or no one tried to deter her from him. The only thing that he couldn't

rob was her job since it wasn't any threat to him. Leon's obsession led him to believe that he would be the only one with access to my mother's mind and heart because he knew it was the only way to control her.

Over the years, I watched the way Leon abused the love my mother had for him. I saw how he used it to his advantage. She clearly couldn't see the negative impact Leon made in our lives because he exposed her to a lavish lifestyle, a life that a country girl wasn't used to. She felt nothing was wrong in their relationship even though she was being robbed by Leon. I felt Leon's dysfunctional love tricked my mother into receiving him with open arms. I hated him with a passion because he conned his way between our bonding times. He was just like a robber taking things that didn't belong to him. The chances of me growing up in a non-dysfunctional home were taken away by him during my childhood years, and the opportunity of me bonding with Jean became a struggle.

Do I think Leon really cared enough about the growth of our relationship? Nope. Not one bit.

In Leon's world, he only cared about his selfish desires and twisted ego.

This unhealthy love contaminated my mother's thoughts, having her to believe Leon was the best thing that ever happened. Leon made sure to run every man out of her life who showed interest. Loving the wrong man made it hard for Jean to appreciate God's gift... Me. She was a prime example of running behind a man who deterred her from seeing what really mattered. If I could describe how I felt, I would say that our relationship wasn't at the top of her to-do-list. Jean was so in love with Leon that it caused her to fall for something that was destined to be meaningless. My mother decided to sacrifice, not knowing her child's birth father for self-satisfaction-- a craving for love from a wealthy man. In fact, Jean thought I would've been the one to keep the relationship going between them both. Sadly, she was the one who caused them to have an up and down relationship. The very thing my mother hoped for, wanting Leon as my birth father, was the one thing that separated the both of them.

As I reflect back, I can say that the entire seven years was like a long roller coaster ride for all of us. If you would ask me whether the ride was worth it, I would respond that we should have picked a ride with less speed. I was left with a headache and ready to vomit all over the place. Honestly, I think a toddler ride would have been a better choice.

Growing up, I learned to take things slowly and pray. God's timing will allow relationships to build into a strong foundation. My mother, on the other hand, had to learn that a baby couldn't keep a man or make him truly love you. When situations like this happen, you understand the difference between love and lust. You learn that real love doesn't hurt or make you be someone other than yourself.

My life in the projects…

The busier my mother became, the more she needed a baby sitter. As a single parent, my mother had to work two jobs to sustain the household bills and take care of her children.

As for James, he was over the falling for Jean's love tricks. He realized that drama wasn't far when it came to co-parenting. Over time, he outsmarted my mother by learning all of her conning, seductive ways. He fed her with a long spoon to keep down confusion by giving her the same amount of money every month. The money barely helped due to my mother's big girl bills. She had the type of bills that required two people to maintain, but Jean's impeccable skills allowed her to make a way out of no way. When she set her mind to a task, it wasn't long before she accomplished what was in her mind to do. The good thing about James and Jean is they remained good friends. In the meantime, Leon disappeared for a while, but wasn't too far to be reached.

If Jean needed extra help, she asked her twenty-two-year old cousin Toya to watch me. Toya also lived in the projects. Everyone knew her to be hot in the pants. If a dude had power or money, Toya wasn't far. She liked the finer things in life and did whatever to get them.

Although there was a lot of shooting and fighting in those days in my neighborhood, I felt the most free. I was taught to be grown before my time. I learned how to dance and dress stylishly from my cousin Toya. She taught me how to be more girly in a mature way. I was her shadow, implementing everything she did. Toya was very wild for her age; the grown folks called it *being fast*. She had a name and that name wasn't a good one. She tried to fit in with the crowd, but went about it the wrong way. As I continued to be around Toya, I found myself in front of little boys' faces when I should've been in the house reading a book.

At times, we rode the bus to the mall to steal clothes with her friends and see this man she called her boyfriend. I didn't like him because every time we visited, he made Toya stay in the room and all I heard was strange noises from the both of them. Every time I heard them moaning, I left his house to play with the neighbor's children who lived two houses down.

Unfortunately, one night didn't go as planned. Like any other visit, he walked us to the bus stop. Normally, I walked ahead so they could be alone but, this time, I heard a loud scream. When I turned around, Toya was getting hit by her boyfriend. When she broke loose, she was able to run; we both ran towards the bus stop.

The bus was coming as we ran away from him. I was scared and started yelling, "Stop... stop... please stop... help!" Luckily, the driver stopped when she saw me running and flagging my arms on the side of the road.

My heart raced from the time we got on the bus to when we made it back to the projects. Toya told me not to tell a soul, so I kept the truth to myself. When my mother came to pick me up, she saw that Toya had a black eye. The first thing my mother wanted to know was whether everyone was alright. Toya's mother pulled my mother to the side and told her that some girls jumped Toya. I looked at Toya, and she looked at me with confusion glazing across her face. I felt badly for her because she was a lost girl. Both of our parents fell for her lie, so my mother decided to let Toya get her car while she worked so that we wouldn't have to walk alone at night. The truth is that having a car only made matters worse.

Toya knew how to trick our parents, so she waited for everything to die down before driving my mother's car. My mother helped Toya get to the very thing she loved the most... trouble. It was as if Toya was only attracted to

"Bad Boys," men known for not taking mess from no one, yet Toya felt excluded from that category. She felt she could say what she wanted. One thing I am sure of: Toya knew how to piss anyone off with her rambling tongue.

One afternoon, Toya wanted to meet up with another guy. He was a drug dealer who lived in this area called *The Horse Shoe*. He lived close by a park that wasn't too far from the projects. The area was known for killings and drug trafficking. If you weren't getting into fights or running from gun shots, then you weren't a part of the hood. Bodies always popped up somewhere; people in that community saw the police yellow tape so much that it felt normal.

I can recall being in the mix of a gun shooting. All of it began when Toya drove to Horse Shoe, where her guy was known to be. As we rode, I looked out the window and saw the kids playing in the park. Toya had the music up loud so that everyone could see her driving a car. I stayed in the car when I saw guys with guns in their hands and some cuffed behind their backs. Like any other time, it didn't take long for them to start cussing each other out. When Toya noticed him reaching for his gun from behind, she rushed back into the car and drove off really fast but decided to drive back around the corner. Toya started cussing at him outside of the window while driving and he began to shoot towards the car; it scared Toya so badly that she pressed down on the gas pedal and drove off speeding. When she turned left, the car tilted on two wheels. I squeezed my seat belt tightly with my eyes opened wide; it felt like my eyelids were touching my forehead. I was in the back seat and all I remember hearing were gun shots while looking down at the road that was a couple of feet from my face.

People who were outside ran into their duplex for safety and called people from the house phone. News travelled fast, but not fast enough. My mother was so clueless about Toya's immature ways that she said nothing to her. I wanted my mother to go off on Toya like some grown lady in the streets. I wanted to know that if I was ever in danger, my mother would protect me. I feel the only reason Toya stopped watching me was because her mother couldn't control her anymore. She started running away, and when that happened, my mother had to reach out to someone else. I couldn't wait to get away from Toya and her boy issues. Toya wasn't all that bad but having to look over my shoulders time-after-time wasn't a great feeling.

My mother's other option was taking me to my great Aunt Lauren, who lived in the same projects. Aunt Lauren knew everyone's business, including the situation with Toya. It wasn't hard to find, out since the streets flooded her business around through the town. In so many ways, Aunt Lauren tried to warn my mother by telling her, "Toya's ass is too fast to be a babysitter."

For some reason, people's ears channeled towards Aunt Lauren; they loved hearing all the juicy gossip. I really believed she should've been a news reporter because there was nothing she didn't know. Every time I turned around, someone was telling her or she was telling someone something. Truthfully, a door opened that should have stayed closed between my Aunt Lauren and mother; instead, they rambled on until all the juice ran out. If you ask me, my mother instantly turned into "Ms. Noise." Hearing all the stories about Toya put my mother in a weird position, causing her to take me to work with her until she found a reliable sitter.

Forced to be something I'm not...

Needless to say, on the way to work, my mother started dropping me off at my Aunt Lauren's apartment. She realized it was only a matter of time before her boss would start complaining about me being on her job. The lobby could only look after me for so long. So, my mother arranged with Aunt Lauren to keep an eye on me until she got off work.

Aunt Lauren cussed like a sailor, but that didn't stop me from wanting to go to her place for some good old fashion cooking. She was shocked to learn about my big appetite. It was nothing for me to ask for seconds. After a couple of times of me asking, Aunt Lauren fixed my plate like she was feeding a grown man. She loved it! She didn't mind feeding children in the projects because she enjoyed cooking. And I didn't mind either! Everything I ate was just delicious. I mean everything.

I watched Aunt Lauren closely since I was confused about her occupation, yet I learned a lot from Aunt Lauren. She was a hustler who made her money in many ways, especially when her clients came to get their hair done. Her salon was her dining room table. She made sure to set everything on her left side since she was left handed. During that time, portable dryers were made like a plastic cap. The plastic cap was connected to a plastic pipe that blew out hot air. It inflated the plastic cap enough to circulate the hot air around to dry the hair. This was one of the ways my Aunt Lauren got all the latest news in the city. My cousins and I knew that when Auntie had a client come over, it was girl talk time.

Boy... oh boy...

They gossiped about everything and everybody.

I knew when the conversation was going to be a long one because the whole apartment had a funky smell. I hated when clients requested that wet and wavy look. We automatically knew a headache, watery eyes and a runny nose were coming. If you're too young to understand what I'm talking about, a wet and wavy look is better known as a Jerry Curl. When a client wanted a wet and wavy look, Auntie draped the client with extra towels and wrapped this long cotton around their heads. Then, she divided the hair into thin sections, wrapped it inside a thin paper strip and rolled it into gray rollers. Once all that was done, Auntie poured a clear liquid on each roller. The smell that came from that bottle had the whole house smelling awful. It was a strong chemical and opened your nostrils to an entirely different level.

Aunt Lauren was known for being the cookie lady too. Everyone in the projects knocked on her door to buy themselves a treat. I felt safer with my aunt when it was just us and my baby cousin Taylor. My Aunt Lauren had full custody over Ashley because her father passed away from AIDS. I didn't know what HIV/AIDS was at that time. I just saw how it made your skin and body change over a period of time. I was able to spend time with her father for a season. I remember that he was always in good spirits until his last days. I could tell he didn't want to suffer any more. When he passed, my cousin told me he visited her one night after his death and said he was going to be alright. She took it better than most children who had lost a parent. My heart was really sad for her because I could tell she was missing her father. We had become really close, so it was fun going over to my Aunt's apartment until my boy cousin came.

A couple of months went by and I was about nine years old when my oldest boy cousin Chase started living with my Aunt Lauren. Everything was fine until I was left alone with him. He exposed me to a world before my time, a world that will break you mentally, leaving you feeling empty and confused. It escalated when he touched me in places a little boy shouldn't touch his relative. His uncircumcised inner demon built enough confidence by manipulating me into lying down so that he could lay his body on top of mine while our clothes were on. When he finished, he threatened to tell my mother what happened if I didn't continue to do what he wanted. I was clueless with everything that took place at that time. I wasn't taught that type of behavior.

I didn't recall asking to be put in a situation like that during my childhood years. To be honest, the moment made me feel it was all my fault for him acting out his sexual teenage habits. I became an introvert when he felt the need to touch me. I just laid in shame and resentment. Since he was a fourteen-year-old boy, Chase's body was going through hormonal changes. When his curiosity arose, Chase decided to take his sexuality to another level. My Aunt Lauren went to the store, so we were left alone in the apartment. On this particular day, Chase's little horny demon wanted to come out to be entertained. Ordinarily, to make that happen, Chase made sure that Aunt Lauren was good and gone. He walked over to his window, opened it and yelled at his two young friends to peek in and watch oral sex being performed on him. Chase wanted to fit into the crowd in every way possible and didn't care who got hurt.

Meanwhile, I was in the living room on the black loveseat watching cartoons. My Aunt's décor arrangement was like the traditional black culture setup with the three-piece black furniture set coordinated with gold and white accessories, the bible character paintings on the wall, the entertainment, television stand and a black coffee table with elephants underneath with their booties facing a certain way. Let me not forget about the plastic mat on the floor that you better walk on to keep from dirtying the carpet. When my Aunt decided to step out, she reminded us that her place better look just like she left it. I made sure to stay in one spot that day until she came back, not knowing that little horny demon was whispering something dirty in Chase's ear.

> Then Chase came walking towards the love seat looking at me all weird.

> In a demanding tone, Chase said, "Heyyyyy! Come in the room."

Since I didn't move fast enough, he pulled me from the living room. I stumbled and tripped a couple of times in the hallway into his bedroom. After he shifted around, he told me to get on my knees. I bent down slowly with a confused look on my face. I knew at this point that nothing good was going to come out of this situation since his hormones were racing. Chase's desire of putting his penis into my mouth was about to be a dream come true for him, but a nightmare for me. I didn't know any better. If I did, I would've done what most little girls do and that's call on my daddy. In my mind, I did, but he didn't come to rescue his little princess.

Instead, I looked at Chase with teary eyes as I watched him pull down his pants. I looked around and saw dirty clothes on the floor, a couple of his tennis shoes tucked under his bunk bed and football posters on a white wall. We were by the room door next to the dresser when he used his left hand to force me to kneel all the way down. With nervousness flowing through my body, I opened my mouth with my eyes closed. Part of me knew what he was doing was wrong while the other part of me felt it was my fault for letting it happen.

This experience made me watch my innocence go straight out the door. I felt lonely, unclean and, most importantly, worthless. I became a statue. I showed no movement. My teeth grazed slightly too hard, making it an uneasy moment for him. After hearing giggles, I opened my eyes when a warm, nasty liquid entered my mouth. Suddenly, I realized the liquid was his urine. I gagged and spit it out right on his pants.

His friends laughed as they ran off. Feeling ashamed and embarrassed, I rushed to the bathroom sink to rinse my mouth out with water. Chase ran behind me to see if I was alright. I rinsed my month over and over. When he touched my shoulder, I looked up at him with an evil look. Inside, I was feeling a rage of hate towards him and wanted every bad thing to happen to him for what he did to me. He changed an innocent girl into a broken soul.

And all I could say to myself was, "Why me?"

"It was like misery was the drug; my past was the dealer and the way I would find the dealer was through my thoughts."
--Shupier Jones

4

BROKEN INTO MANY PIECES

How can you fix something that's been broken? You may say it depends on what is broken. If it's glass, wood, steel, or plastic, those things can be easily fixed by using glue. Now allow yourself to dig deeper in thought to imagine that very broken thing is you. Sometimes, fixing a broken object can be tricky, but trying to put a human back together is challenging. If you ask me, it depends on what part of you is broken. I don't want you to get confused when I say "broken" because I'm not talking about broken bones.

When I refer to broken, I'm referring to a broken heart, mind, and spirit. I don't care how hard you try to go on with life, if these things aren't in line, trust and believe that it will show. Being broken can and will change who God created you to be. For instance, when you're broken, fear takes a stand on your journey to success, causing you to become afraid and lose focus on achieving greatness. When you're emotional while making decisions, your thinking becomes unstable in critical moments, causing you to be involved in deadly situations that only God Almighty can help you get out of.

I can label all the bad when it comes to be being broken, but later in life, I learned that the Most High uses the broken. He uses the one who has been through struggles, hurt, pain, loss, and loneliness so that they can help those in similar situations. This is one reason I am happy that I went though some things. You may ask, "Why?" My answer is, "To be used by the one who created me, the one who can win every war and overcome every situation, Christ." In this chapter, you will understand my feelings, thoughts, and experiences during the times I really felt broken.

As you have read, my experiences as a child weren't happy go lucky. My childhood broke me down mentally and physically. I went into a shell to hide my pain so that no one could see how broken I was on the inside. You would've thought I was just some quiet child raised to be respectful, but I was a walking puzzle waiting for someone to put me back together. Of course, I went about it the wrong way. Instead of depending on GOD, I looked for people to piece me back together.

When you are a child, you go to the person you feel the most comfortable with, such as a parent, sibling, grandparent, Pastor, God-parent, or childhood friend. During this particular time, I was too young to understand that GOD could save me from the very thing designed to destroy me. I went to church; I heard about Him, but not enough to say that I knew the MOST HIGH power. I was 10 years old and leaning on my own understanding, which led me to bondage. In so many words, I felt there was no hope for me. The more I closed in, the worse it got; it was so bad that I started feeling depressed and lonely at the same time. I wanted my mother to understand; instead, she was too busy trying to figure out her issues.

I was lonelier than anything, and it didn't help being different from all the other children. I realized at a young age that I didn't fit in with the rest of the crowd, especially the more popular girls in elementary school.

In all honesty, I felt like Dorothy from the *Wizard of Oz*, when the storm carried her to an unfamiliar place. Even though I wasn't transported in a house per se, a storm caused me to live in another location that I knew very little about. Let's not bring up the *Yellow Brick Road and those red slippers;* I can only begin to imagine how Dorothy felt walking with a bunch of strangers on an unfamiliar road wearing uncomfortable church looking shoes. The *Wizard of Oz* storyline happens somewhat all the time to people. Think of it like this, people relocate all the time due to a career, educational or family situation. I know because Hurricane Andrew disintegrated the south part of Florida; because of that, my mother had to send me away.

The storm blew me away, but not to a yellow brick road...

On August 11, 1992, South Florida was hit by a category five hurricane that injured and killed many people plus destroyed homes, schools, and workplaces. In this case, I was forced to live with my Aunt Tina for a year. The transition wasn't that hard for me because every summer break, I stayed with her. In fact, it worked out perfectly for my mother because I was in north Florida when the storm appeared. My mother was home at the time of the storm. She later told me that she hid in her closet for safety. The windows were covered with hurricane shutters and the house was made of brick. My mother was grateful to be alive given that the closet was the only place where the roof didn't cave in.

Although the storm seemed like a curse to most, to some, it was a blessing in disguise. My mother was one of the fortunate ones who purchased homeowner's insurance. Many people had to depend on the government for assistance in healthcare and shelter. However, my mother's insurance company sent someone immediately to begin the process of restoring her home. She had no hassle with the insurance company when the agent inspected the house; in fact, the agent signed a check the same day for a nice amount. My mother made the right decision by using the money wisely; she positioned herself by boosting and reconstructing her life on a different level. My mother knew it would take time to get back on track so she set goals, stayed focused and provided all the necessities for her children.

There's no place like home...

Living with Aunt Tina wasn't that bad in the beginning. She was married to my Uncle William, and they had two children. Even though my Aunt's older child wasn't my Uncle's daughter, you couldn't tell because he treated her as if she was his very own. My Aunt was very short with silky, dark skin that had no trace of acne. She was a little thicker than my mother. Her hair was always straightened because she used a hot comb. In those days, blacks were more prone to using hair grease, a stove and a metal comb than using what they called hair crack, which is another name for a relaxer. My little cousin and I were lucky because our aunt used a kiddie relaxer to maintain the texture of our hair. We were happy because we didn't have to experience grease burning our scalp or a hot comb touching our ears.

For the most part, Aunt Tina was the type of woman who would do anything for her loved ones until the other person came out called, "The Beast." If truth be told, the beast wasn't nothing nice either. Please don't come to a hasty conclusion when I reference her to a beast. She, like most women, will defend the ones she deeply cares about and herself. If I must, I will define her as one of those so called... beasty women. That doesn't take much from any one.

Wait! Wait! I can't forget to tell you that Aunt Tina was a compulsive liar, the funny type! The crazy thing is the family knew it. When they did catch on to the lie, it would be a week later, but they all just laughed! It was hard for you to get mad at her when you finally caught onto

Tina's lies. Her lies just seemed real; even with the possibility of knowing, what she said could be a lie, you still wanted to believe her because what Aunt Tina said seemed so realistic. The funny part is that she found it humorous to convince people that her lies were true; it was her way of joking around with the family.

Don't get me wrong, Aunt Tina had a lot of great qualities. For instance, she made sure the house was in order and that we always had a hot meal on the table, clean clothes, transportation to and from school and lived in a safe environment. I remember the bathroom closet was filled with hygiene and cleaning supplies. We never ran out of soap, lotion, toothpaste, shampoo, conditioner, hair products or cleaning products. She took from stores a lot; sometimes, we helped her. We were in the store stealing with Aunt Tina, but we didn't know any better; it was normal for us to put things in the bag and walk out the store without paying for them. All Aunt Tina cared about was surviving and taking care of her family the best way she knew how. Also, there wasn't too much you could get over on her. Aunt Tina noticed that every time her sisters came over, her stock of products was missing.

"I'm going to fix these heffas," said Tina.
She got them alright! One thing you didn't want to do was piss off Aunt Tina. You could only get over her head so many times. That's why she put a lock on the door to stop her sisters from taking products from out the closet. When she came into town, my mother was the only sister allowed in the closet. There were certain privileges the siblings showed my mother because she was the oldest.

The only thing you could probably get from Aunt Tina was her famous out of the box brownies. She made the best tasting brownies you could ever eat. After they were fully cooked, she'd cut the brownies like you would slice pizza. It made you feel like you were getting more when she cut them like a triangle rather than a square. I think the trick to it tasting so well was how she would whip all the ingredients together. The batter looked creamy when she poured it into the round metal pan. Once the brownies were cool enough to eat, they went quickly.

Be careful what you ask for...

Eventually, I had to start elementary school since the summer break was coming to an end and fourth grade was knocking at the back door. I attended a school called Eastside Elementary. Some of my happiest days came from attending this school. The first couple days of school seemed rough since I didn't know anybody except my younger cousin, who was much younger than me. Luckily, I met a girl named Charlie who later became one of my closest friends. She was the type of child who made boys as friends very easily. She was more like a tomboy, so the boys didn't mind her hanging around.

One day, I was sitting down in the stands when Charlie ran over to me with a soccer ball in her hand during recess time.

She asked, "Hey, What's your name?"

I replied, "Ronesha."

"You're not from here, huh?" Charlie asked.

I looked at her while placing my right hand over my forehead to block the sunlight from getting into my eyes. I smirked then shook my head and responded, "Not really, I was born here, but I was raised in Miami."

"Cool, I heard about Miami. I heard a lot of killing goes on down there," Charlie said then asked, *"You want to play some soccer with us? We need one more person on our team!"*

With a shocked look on my face, I answered, "Who me?"

Sarcastically, Charlie responded, "No, I am talking to the invisible person sitting next to you! Who else you think I'm talking to? Do you wanna play or not?"

I said loudly, "Yes, I want to play!"

I stood up slowly and stepped over the bleachers. As I looked up at her, she answered with excitement, "Come on then!"

Seconds later, I kicked the soccer ball so hard it instantly caused her to realize I had athletic skills and didn't mind getting dirty with the boys. I had so much fun that day. Charlie was so happy too because she finally met a girl with the same athletic abilities.

Since that day, Charlie and I played every sport together. We were inseparable, like two peas in a pod. Our differences became a great mixture and developed into a chemistry some will never encounter in a real friendship. I was the quiet ladybug while Charlie was the social butterfly. Charlie was one of the more popular girls whereas I was known as the quiet, new girl on the block. Everyone loved Charlie, and if they didn't like her, it was because they were jealous of her character. At times, we competed against each other in a healthy way. The type of competitiveness we had wasn't to tear each other down but to make us play better in whatever sport we chose. Charlie was one of the first friends I recall having who didn't try to mentally hurt me. Those were some good moments since I didn't really have my mother or father around.

I got exactly what I didn't want...

Staying with my Aunt and Uncle wasn't all that bad because more minor than severe situations happened in this small town. Like any other family, my Aunt and Uncle faced very few issues. They had the type of conflicts that were easy to bounce back from since their differences weren't feasible enough to travel around town.

In one case, news started traveling about my Uncle William cheating with another woman. He knew when that gossip got to the wrong person that his business would be known by everyone. At this point, all he could do was hope that more news didn't get added to it. Sad to say, Uncle William's name was the talk of the town; people floated the gossip around and everything you could think made it bigger than it was. My Aunt's sisters kept telling her about her husband. One day, her emotions rushed rapidly, so it didn't take her long to start investigating what people were spreading around town. Of course, my Aunt played it cool at first, but when she had solid information on the other woman; she was ready to go to war.

Aunt Tina didn't tolerate foolishness when it came to her family or money.

Repeatedly, Aunt Tina asked Uncle William about the other woman, but he denied it was true. When she confronted him again months later, he had to explain why she kept hearing her husband being called a low down dirty dog. In the middle of them arguing, my Uncle had the slightest idea of how fed up Aunt Tina was with his cheating habits. Since my Aunt was at her breaking point, the beast cage finally broke open; it was only a matter of time before she would explode. As the rage increase, Aunt Tina released the beast from the inside to destroy the target---William. Without being warned, she began knocking at Mr. Homicide's back door; luckily, he did not answer.

My cousin and I were with our neighbors at bible study the night Aunt Tina had her last straw. A fight started between my Aunt and Uncle; Aunt Tina's inner beast came on the scene. William thought he was a match for Tina, a scarred woman who felt betrayed and heartbroken. This particular day, Uncle

William couldn't talk his way out of the situation, not even the blood from his body could defend him. Tina's pain took over and made her black out from really being able to control her actions.

Aunt Tina pushed William in the chest several times; he stretched his arms outward to prevent physical contact between them. It seemed the more unruffled, he remained; the more destructive she wanted to become.

"Move woman," William said calmly while pushing her out of his way.

Aunt Tina squeezed his right arm tightly to pull him back towards her, replying in an aggressive tone, "After all the shit I did for you, you had to go fuck around on me; I hate you!"

They both scuffed back and forth then Uncle William got in Aunt Tina's face, saying, "Here you go again, throwing in my face what you done for me. All you do is run your got damn mouth woman! I'm done with this... shit!"

She responded, "Fuck you asshole!

Aunt Tina stumbled onto the floor when Uncle William used both of his hands to break away from her. Suddenly, she had a flashback of all the agony he put her through. She breathed heavily as her chest vibrated from her heart, beating faster. Her palms became sweaty, and before the sweat fell from her forehead, the beast began to unfold. Her bottled emotions had no barrels anymore; they began to filter out like soda coming out of its bottle after being shaken.

When she realized she was on the floor, Aunt Tina used the right side of her body to lift up towards the end of the counter to pick herself back up. She then turned back towards Uncle William while her untamable thoughts reminded her of all her silent tears and sleepless nights. At this point, she was ready to seek revenge. She wanted William to feel the same pain she felt. She moved quickly and started punching him in the back. Seconds later, William pushed her against the counter in the kitchen. Aunt Tina looked around until her eyes concentrated on the black handled knife. William held her by the arms with extra pressure, ground his teeth together, took a deep breath, released her arms and said, "Enough woman, I am not trying to hurt you!"

He let her go and turned around to walk away. Once she noticed his focus was no longer on her, Aunt Tina reached over to grab the butcher knife from the dish rack. With an evil look in her eyes, she glanced at him, saying, "You're not going anywhere!"

Aunt Tina grew angrier while holding the knife in her hand and sliced her husband on the back of his neck. She dropped the knife on the floor. Though the blood from his body squirted everywhere, Aunt Tina kept fighting William. She released all the bottled emotions, and her inner beast continued to attack him... the prey.

In the meantime, the next-door neighbor heard them yelling back and forth and took no time to call the cops. Later, all I heard were the sirens coming from the police cars and ambulance truck. Aunt Tina snapped back to her senses and saw blood everywhere on the kitchen floor and walls. She dropped to the floor, laying in denial and feeling numb to what she just did to her husband. When the investigators arrived, one went to the front door and an officer went to the back of the house. The officer who went to the back saw the back door slightly cracked; he knocked three times and said, "Lake City P.D! Is anyone home?"

He peeked in and saw a body on the floor and a woman on her knees leaning against the wall in a daze. He immediately called for backup on his radio and rushed inside to check my uncle's pulse to see if he was still alive.

> He looked towards my aunt, saying, "Ma'am, are you hurt? Do you need the ambulance?"

Tina answered the officer in silence while staring at my uncle's body. After investigators got her to talk, the evidence gathered showed the fight took place in the kitchen where Aunt Tina grabbed the knife to slice my Uncle in the back of his neck. Since he was losing too much blood from the womb, William was rushed in the ambulance to the hospital for immediate care. The cut nearly cost Uncle William his life. Aunt Tina was blessed. God works in mysterious ways, or should I say, "HE works behind the scenes."

In fact, my cousin and I were at church when all this occurred. We were clueless about what lied ahead of us. On our way from church, we noticed red and blue lights coming from our street. When the van turned on the street, we couldn't help but look like we had seen a ghost when the van stopped in front of my Aunt's house next to a police officer.

The officer flashed his light inside the van saying, "Sir and Ma'am, keep moving your vehicle. You all cannot stop here."

Our white neighbor pointed towards the back seat and responded with a concerned look on his face, "Well Officer, excuse me sir, the two young ladies that we have in the car live here. My wife and I are bringing them back home from Wednesday night church service. What will you like for us to do with them?"

The officer lifted his right hand and directed the neighbor to move the van onto the side of the road. As the van moved, I looked out the window and saw police cars in front of the house. I was so scared; I did not know what was happening or where my Aunt and Uncle were. All I remembered seeing were cops with flashlights in their hands as they walked back and forth into the house, people standing on the side of the road whispering amongst each other and flashing red and blue lights. Finally, the officer returned with a family member, and we left with my mother's other sister, Aunt Karla.

My mother was called by phone and given a full rundown by her siblings on what happened between Tina and William. It didn't take her long to get on the highway to head towards Lake City, Florida.

This experience almost cost Aunt Tina life in prison, but luckily, the judge only gave her less than three years of time. The good part was my uncle didn't die; hopefully, he learned from this life changing experience. Most importantly, I learned to not mistreat someone who truly loves you. It's not right to lead on or lie to a person who has your best interest at heart. I really enjoyed my days with them. I felt badly about how everything ended. I was just beginning to adapt to my new environment. Plus, I had to go back home with my mother to a place that was no longer the same due to the storm.

They say be careful what you ask for because you may not be ready for it when it comes. I wanted to be back home with my mother, but I don't think she was quite ready for me. In this case, she didn't have much of a choice but to take me back with her to Miami. I was well on my way to walking this yellow brick road of mine after all with a sad face, saying," There's no place like home."

Now, you may be curious about my next experiences, thoughts and feelings. Just know it doesn't stop here. Let's fast forward into my teenage years.

"If you allow a piece of clothing to define who you are, then you'll never reach your greatest potential in the very skin you wear."
--Shupier Jones

5

THE CRUTCHES REMOVED FROM UNDER MY ARMS

Depending on someone for your happiness is the worst thing a person can do. Do you agree? If your answer is yes, you probably encountered a moment where you allowed people to validate when you were in good spirits. Most of the time when you give a person that type of access, you're prone to being mistreated. If you're not careful, they will screw you up and spit you out like that black piece of candy you accidently ate out of the jellybean jar, the black one that most people pick across because of its nasty taste. That same awful taste can surface when you've allowed someone the freedom to dictate your mood. This is a sign of a powerless person who clearly has no self-control in his or her emotions, thoughts or body language. I deeply believe you can build a strong connection in letting a person become your crutch because you relied on them to help you function through moments you believed brought you happiness. I was once that powerless person who used crutches on a weekly basis. If I may describe the meaning of crutches, I will reference a person full of pain, which hides behind and leans on others instead of letting go of the past hurt so they can walk and function into their purpose.

In this chapter, you will understand I was once that individual who depended on people to function as my crutch instead of removing a generational habit of mine. In addition, you will understand how it stagnated my thought process and cluttered my mind with double mindedness until the crutches were removed. It's so important for you to be careful what you absorb as a child. I strongly support that statement for these simple reasons: my past feelings, thoughts and experiences were clouded with hurtful moments. I had no idea past encounters left me feeling mentally crippled. When all alone, I was able to walk.

If you're saying, "I'm this person. Now, how do I know I'm letting someone be my crutch and How do I stop it?" Please, allow me to explain my life experiences using crutches.

After the fight, we became two peas in a pod

For the most part, the 1990's were considered the good old days. Around this time, more people got along than in this day and time. If you were a single parent, it was easy to get an old lady to watch your kids while you worked. Plus, back then, children didn't go hungry because families cooked enough food for the entire block. You hardly saw families going through the drive thru to pick up breakfast or dinner. I recall witnessing more unity than hate back then.

Stepping into this era ended up being my best years as an adolescent. I moved back to the same house the hurricane damaged. The positive outcome of this whole situation was a lot of the homes were basically new after being rebuilt. My grandfather was a construction worker, so it was easy for my mother to contact him to fix any damages in her home. When he started working on the roof, we stayed in a small trailer parked in the front of the house for a couple of months until the house was finished. My mother was very fortunate to have someone with a validated license to work on the house since a lot of scams were going on in the area.

When summer ended, a lot of reconstruction was going on around town, but that didn't stop the school system from re-opening schools. I went to elementary school on the opposite side of town by the projects in Naranja, Fl. You can only imagine how that might have been during that time. Truthfully, having to attend school with children from the projects on top of learning a few things from my mother taught me how to adapt in any environment or setting. Children who come from the projects were some of the most talented people and their parents knew it, so they constantly pushed their child even harder to be better in life. Truth be told, the storm had a lot to do with it; it allowed many to learn how to hustle for what they want out of life, survive, and face their deepest fear. I learned that only the strong survive when placed in the toughest situations. If you were what they called "being lame" in these streets, you failed every time. Honestly, the weak side of me went through a training process, but it didn't take me long to come out strong as a whistle.

Moving back to the city of Miami was like starting all over again, and I mean it when I say that I didn't need a fresh start. I stand firm on that because it seemed like every time I went to a different location, something bad happened. The type of mentality I had as an adolescent was, *if it's broke, don't fix it*. Although I could've labeled myself as the broken also, I felt unfixable. When you really think about it, no matter how super the glue is, the object will never have its natural strength; in fact, it will break again if it's not handled with delicacy.

The comparison in all of this is the broken "object" was me and the "help" is the glue. If your foundation is broken, you will definitely need to be renovated soon. If you choose to ignore it, eventually you'll stop believing your existence has a purpose. When I returned to Miami, my foundation was full of cracks with a little strength left but not enough to handle the storms coming my way. When you endure these type of experiences, it makes you crumble; moreover, you feel forced to rely on crutches (another person) to hold you up to walk this path called life. I don't want you to misunderstand about leaning on someone; it's alright to lean on someone from time-to-time, but draining them with your problems on a regular basis is an issue.

The person I laid most of my weight (problems) on was a girl named Commelina. I met Commelina once in third-grade, again in fifth grade, but it wasn't until middle school that she became my best friend. She was like my on-call therapist; listening to every problem I had, no matter whether I repeated them over and over. It was funny that a kid fight actually allowed us to cross each other's paths. Commelina looked like an antique china doll, the ones the owner leaves inside a glass display case because it is just too beautiful to touch. She was mixed with two different cultures: African American and Hispanic, which produced her skin tone, and her long black hair that was always kept in ponytails. Around this time, Commelina was her mother's only child, so there wasn't anything she couldn't get as a child. Even though she resided in the projects, her mother kept her well-dressed in cute girly clothes. She was so beautiful that High School teenage boys couldn't wait until she got a little older. They saw the potential of her becoming an attractive young lady due to her body figure being shaped like a young woman.

A few months before the storm came; we connected for a brief moment in the girl's restroom on Naranja Park. It was the beginning of summer on a very hot day, and it seemed like everybody was in the park this particular day. Some kids were playing in the community pool and some in the park. I remember this day clearly; the truth is that it's kind of hard to forget a time when you were the laughingstock. This is the time I connected with Commelina, a person who showed me that loyalty will show through regardless if you know a person or not.

After playing for a little while in the park, I saw a sky-blue car pull up next to the playground. The car door opened then a hand reached for the side of the door and there she was: a beautiful chocolate little girl with long rich black hair that stopped in the middle of her back. She wore her favorite colorful flower jump suit with white sandals strapped around her ankles. Commelina got out the car fully, closed the door and waved goodbye to her mother as she drove off. Instantly, her beauty became the center of attention. Every young boy's focus turned towards her so that they forgot about the rest of the girls playing on the playground. But, everyone knew not to say too much to her because of her daddy, Big Cane Jr. In those days, when two young children liked each other, they called it puppy love, and it was major if you both kissed. You knew that if you both got caught kissing, your parents would tear your behind up. Well, I experienced the kissing thing with one of the most popular boys in the neighborhood, yet I noticed I didn't have his attention anymore when Commelina came on the scene. Part of me was hurt and the other part of me felt angry. I wasn't in the mood to accept the rejection from the little boy who gave me my first kiss. My reaction turned into anger when I tried playing with him. From the looks of it all, his way of doing things wasn't allowing me to calm down until he stopped ignoring me and taking his focus off Commelina.

Feeling rejected and hurt that he couldn't say two words, before I knew it, I had grabbed him by the neck with both of my hands and choked him at the top of the slide. We tussled back and forth against the plastic wall at the top of the play house. He was so scared that he slapped me on the right side of my face to let him loose. It worked. I took a couple of steps backwards to balance myself, but when I looked him in the eyes, I became teary-eyed. He was short of breath. He placed both of his hands on his knees to catch his breath. All of a sudden, every child rushed over to where we were to see what was going on saying, "Fight! Fight!"

I looked at them with my hand on my face, feeling embarrassed and confused with what just happened. I was speechless so I jumped down, pushed my way through the crowd of children and ran across the basketball courts headed to the girls' restroom.

> Some of his friends climbed to the top of the slide and stood next to him, laughing at me as I ran off. I was lost on what just happened and not even close to figuring out why I'd behaved that way. Half way away from the playground, his friends started singing loudly, "Fellas there's a jealous girl in our town, ah baby!" Commelina witnessed everything and became concerned. She was so mad at them for singing.
>
> "Ya'll stupid," said Commelina as she ran behind me.

When she came into the restroom, she saw me looking in the mirror checking my face. I touched my face where I'd been hit, reached over and grabbed a napkin to wipe the sweat off my face. I looked in the mirror and saw Commelina looking at me.

She walked slowly towards me and asked, *"Are you okay?"*

I turned my head towards her and said, *"Yeah, I'm okay."*

As we stared at ourselves in the mirror, she looked towards me with a sad face, took her hand and rubbed me cross my back; then she left, walking slowly out the restroom back to the playground. It was hard to forget her because she was the only person who came and checked on me. She had this genuineness about her; she felt like a safe person to be around. Overall, I didn't understand it until two years later when we met again in the fifth grade.

The melody made the connection

In the month of September 1995, I started the fifth grade at Naranja Elementary. My teacher's name was Mrs. Harris. She did not take any bull crap from nobody. She was well-respected in the school system and the community. Very few parents didn't agree with her teaching; if there were any, it was because she disciplined their child. She handled the students considered the worst of the worst; by the end of the school year, that student was well-mannered and ready to learn. Mrs. Harris walked and spoke with authority; her presence demanded respect wherever she went.

Mrs. Harris made a big impact in my life because she prepared me for middle school. At first, I didn't understand why she was placed in my life, but as time progressed, I realized how valuable she was to me. She taught all her students how to become leaders and to be independently inclined. She always preached how minorities should stick together no matter what. Every time we heard her say, "Them, They and Us," we knew it was her inside code that stood for whites, Hispanics and Blacks. She made sure to remind us every day that "Us" need to do better in bettering ourselves. Foolish as it sounded to us, she was absolutely right. What I loved about her the most was she pulled out every great quality she knew her students had within. She showed no mercy; any sign of weakness from her could detour the student away from what they were capable of accomplishing--being a successful leader.

I made sure that I didn't give Mrs. Harris any problems the whole school year. You just knew not to come off disrespectful to Mrs. Harris. To be honest, I was more afraid of her than my mother. Besides, I wanted to be on her good side so I could be a part of the talent show the school had every year. In order to be in the showcase, you must meet certain criteria, such as turning in all of your assignments, maintaining good conduct, having a permission slip signed by your parents to be involved and having a talent. It was the best feeling in the world to have all the requirements needed to be considered one of the talents in the showcase.

One day, auditions were being held, so my best friend and I decided to partner up, trying out as a female R&B singing group. We couldn't wait to show off our skills to the other contestants who came to audition. Unfortunately, another girl group presented the same concept in front of the judges. The talent coordinators felt both groups did an exceptional job so they decided to put both groups together instead of choosing between the four of us. It worked out in our favor for one simple reason: we all carried different voice ranges. There was just one problem: we couldn't figure out a song that we all could agree to sing in the talent show.

A couple of days later, we had our first practice in the cafeteria after school for two hours. As we entered, each student was directed to their assigned table. The other two girls that were a part of the group came in from doing their patrol duties. Before we started, we introduced ourselves by name and did small talk.

> My friend from my class started off first saying, "Hi, my name is Chandrise."
>
> "Hey, my name is Ronesha," I said.
>
> "What's ya'll names?" *I asked the two girls from the other class.*

The first girl, whose skin tone looked caramel, said, "My name is Cindy. We are in Ms. Hernandez class."

The dark-skinned girl said, "Everybody call me Commelina."

I had this strangest feeling come over me when the last girl from the other group said her name. She looked very familiar; I felt like I had seen her from somewhere before. While the girls kept talking, I looked down at the floor and had a flashback of a time when I was in the restroom on Naranja Park. I vaguely remembered the girl from the park because it was two years ago when I last saw of her. With a dumbfounded look, I stared at Commelina who sat across from me. She reminded me of another girl who followed me into the restroom after a boy slapped me in my face in the park. I tried to shake it off, but I was stuck in that moment of time. I realized she may be the little girl who wore that flower jumpsuit that day. She had that long hair, and her voice sounded just like the girl in the restroom. I really wasn't sure and part of me was too embarrassed to bring up that moment.

Meanwhile, I sat in a daze while they debated back and forth about who was going to be the lead singer. The music teacher tried to give us time to figure it out by ourselves, but we ended up wasting an hour not getting anywhere. She knew if she didn't intervene there was going to be a girl war soon.

> Chandrise from my class shook me and said, "Ronesha, the music coordinator is coming over here."

When I came back to reality, I saw her walking towards the table we were sitting at to ask us did we need any help. We told her we were having trouble choosing a song to sing. She looked at all of us and mentioned a female R&B group called Xscape.

> "You ladies can sing their song called Understanding," she stated.

> "Yes," we all responded loudly.

> She said excitedly, "What are you ladies waiting on? Get started, practice is almost over!"

After she walked away crossing her arms with a big smile on her face, it took us no time to begin practicing singing the song all together. At the end of practice, we agreed to practice at my house over the weekend. It wasn't hard for us to pick which singer's part best suited us; all we had to do was match the person according to her voice range.

We practiced away from school in my mother's garage for three weeks so that we could perfect our sound and moves. It inspired us so much that we wanted to become a famous singing group. This was one of the first times I saw my mother being involved in something I was great at doing. Seeing my mother happy made me happy, and her being active made us a better singing group. Having a supportive mom helped me a lot in this part of my journey; it was well needed since we didn't have many moments that were all that great. My mother showed no signs of confusion about her parenting skills. She had great leadership qualities that also helped the other parents adapt well with each other and influenced them to participate in making our group better.

We needed that support from all the mothers because it was something we lacked from a mother figure. In this case, their support made us push harder and feel good to have all our mothers active in our lives. Our mothers ended up being way cooler than we thought. I remember smiling, laughing and joking. We had so much fun when we had all the mothers under the same roof. Our practices even became more intense; our parents really thought that they were our managers and forgot we were just doing a talent show. So when any one of them came around, they made sure to rehearse us like a real R&B group. We sang over and over; they critiqued any wrong moves, motivating us and recording our every move with their video cameras.

The night of the show we wore all black gear: a black top with black jeans and black boots. So many people came to see the students perform that night. Commelina was sad because she was the only one of the group missing her mother. She didn't let that stop her because she caught a ride with another contestant to the show. We all had been waiting for this moment that felt like it took forever, but it finally came; it was time to show the audience our singing and dance skills. We were nervous, but when that music started, every nervous feeling left quickly. We put on a performance that left the audience with a moment they will never forget. When we got to the end of the song, everyone in the crowd gave us a standing ovation. Seeing people cheering at the top of their lungs, clapping and whistling was when we knew that all the hard work paid off. From that moment, all the girls stayed in contact with each other until we went off to middle school.

It was hard saying Goodbye

On Saturday, December 14, 1996, my mother gave me my first teenage birthday party. You could hear the music blasting a few blocks away; it was so loud that the neighbor's walls on the side of us were vibrating from the speakers. I was feeling myself so much that a person couldn't tell me anything the night of my party. In all honesty, I got to feel what it's like to be accepted. I had a new outfit on and knowing that all my friends from school were at my party made me feel great inside.

I became happier when my Spanish boyfriend Jamal came walking in the backyard with his brother and sisters. Everybody knew they were not from our neck of the woods by the way they talk and dressed. I smiled when I rushed over to him and wrapped my arms around his neck to give him a warm hug. I blushed every time I heard the sound of his New York accent; it was the one thing I loved most about him. Our relationship was kept on the low. We made people believe we were just close friends. We kept it that way because getting my mother to approve of us being together wouldn't happen. I was her little girl, so the only thing she wanted me focused on was school books, not boys.

It was hard not to have fun that night; people came from all over the place to my party. I was fortunate that everyone came on their best behavior. Thinking back, I thank God there weren't any fights or gun shootings that night because the whole block was filled with cars and people standing on the side walk. Maybe it had to do with my neighbor being a police officer. Honestly, I cared less about who showed up. My main focus was having a great turn out. I wanted my party to be a night to remember (with a crowd of people in my front and backyard.) If I had any concerns about anything, it was fitting in with the crowd and being thought of as the cool girl at school.

Returning to school, I was the topic of the day for a couple of days until someone else had a party; then, they ended up being the new talk. The circle of peers once around me shifted into a different direction, leaving me hanging. Literally, it started eating me alive because no matter how hard I tried to belong, it didn't work. If I had known then what I know now, it wasn't intended for me to.

Commelina reminded me often that being you is all you needed to focus on. Easy as her words sounded, I made it my business to listen to everything she said as well as give her my full attention but holding on to past hurt didn't allow me to see my true worth. Believe me when I tell you that I listened to her speeches, visualized myself as a confident person and tried to follow through, but for some reason, having low self-esteem was implanted inside my brain. Having this empty void of wanting to be loved kept me infatuated with the feeling of being accepted by others, whether they truly cared or not.

I was blessed to have a person who really cared and knew a side of me that most didn't know existed; my true friend Commelina kept her ears close and a shoulder near when I started to feel depressed. Her loyalty mediated the war between my mind and heart, a battle of differentiating real from fake love. Regardless of any disagreement, she handled our friendship with care. She remained consistent with being honest, loyal and loveable. Eventually, we earned each other's trust and told our dark, deepest secrets. It still was hard telling her, but once the walls came down, it started to help me release myself from childhood hurt. From that experience, Commelina entered into my world, which she wasn't quite familiar with. It was like trusting crutches to hold your body weight while you fear falling as you walk to your destination. I was mentally injured and trying to get through my personal dilemmas, which wasn't happening unless I had Commelina advising me. She was my crutch, and as long as she was there, I stayed in self-pity, which led me to believe I couldn't stand on my own.

Over time, Commelina warned me to stop being so vulnerable because it was easy for people at school to take advantage of me. I was a giver, so I didn't see it as people taking advantage; I viewed it as me being a helper. I was the type who didn't wait for my friends or anyone to ask; if I knew of their need, I had no problem giving. It took a couple of situations to backfire on me to understand that I was being used by people I thought really needed help. When someone turned against me, I contacted Commelina.

In the early 90's, cell phones weren't as popular as today, but it was normal to have a beeper. When Commelina saw the special code come across her screen, she knew to get ready for me to tell her a story about being mistreated. She didn't have a house phone, so she walked across the street to the plaza where the building had a payphone.

Commelina rushed out the house feeling upset; it made her go into defense mode because she hated when people mistreated me. We talked for a couple of minutes, and by the end of the conversation, she would say,

> *"Man, gul-gal don't tell me nothing else, now I want to fight them. You know I don't like when people mistreat you. I told you, to stop being so nice to everyone."*

I replied, "I know I have to stop."

> *After taking a deep breathe, she said, "People don't care! They only care about themselves. I'm about to go home, it's getting dark and I don't want Ma to worry. I will see you in class tomorrow. I love you. Bye-Bye"*

Leaning on the wall in the kitchen, I responded, "I love you too. Goodnight." I hung the phone up and went to my room, feeling resentment towards friends who disappointed me. I stayed up for a while crying until I fell asleep.

As the months flew by, Commelina and I were inseparable; we did everything together like best friends normally did. We were like two peas in a pod. If you didn't know any better, you would have thought she was my biological sister because we had similar features. She just wasn't the athletic type; however, I was the one who loved the mental and physical parts of playing a sport. I played basketball, and we both ran track together but that didn't last for long; eventually, she stopped. But, it didn't stop her from being my personal cheer leader. I could count on her to be sitting in the bleachers yelling and screaming at the top of her lungs when I had a basketball game or track meet. Along with my mother, Commelina was my biggest supporter in middle school.

I learned so many things by being around her; Commelina exposed me to what it was like to live in the hood. I knew something, but by being around Commelina and her family, I learned more. I was once that person ignorant to the hood lifestyle, but she showed me how to react to certain situations if I ever was placed in them. Over all, Commelina came from a family who made due with what they had, so materialistic things weren't their number one priority. She was taught that love and unity were way more important than having things. So, my heart broke into pieces when my best friend left Miami to live with her father in Atlanta, Georgia. I had finally met someone who understood me. I didn't have to worry about being someone else because Commelina accepted me for who I was. It was hard to function without her; I felt lonely all over again. I had no one to else to hide behind when I came against depression. When Commelina moved away, I felt a little off balance. It seemed as though my happiness came then got snatched away right before my very eyes. I felt I would crumble without my crutches.

When one person moves out of your life, more step in...

You can say that it was a good thing that my brother Trevor and my mom's baby sister Caroline moved in with us. They came when I was going into seventh grade, during the summer so that it would be a smooth transition. Both my great-grandmother and granny felt moving them in with my mother would be better because they needed to change their surroundings. It was cool until I had to share my room with Aunt Caroline. My brother and Aunt were a little older than me, so they had to attend High School.

As siblings, Trevor and I weren't close at all; I guess it came from being raised in two different households as children. We got along some of the time, but I struggled with sharing my space at times. I had been the only child for so long; therefore, having to adapt to sharing my personal space with someone else was pretty hard. On the other hand, Caroline found her niche in Miami, FL; she knew how to make friends very quickly but made poor choices when picking guys to date. Her and I got into trouble for getting caught stealing out of the Mall. My mother tore our behinds up. So, if we got into any conflicts, Caroline would leave and hang out with her beautiful chunky light-skinned friend. We called her Calena. Calena's mother found me adorable and always asked me to ride with her when she dropped Calena to our house. Normally, I would say, "No, thank you." I was a homebody, so I didn't like to leave home, but she bribed me by saying she would buy me the color finger nail polish I wanted. I ran in the house so fast to put some shoes on you would've thought I was running a sprint. When I came out of the house, I ran back towards the car and got into the back seat. My mother walked outside to her white car to speak before we left. My aunt and Calena went on the side of the house to the back porch. Meanwhile, Calena's mother was shocked to see me rush to the back seat.

"Little girl, get in this front seat!" said *Calena's mom.*

Jean leaned on her side of the window, responding in a joking way, "She doesn't like sitting in the front seat. She likes to be chauffeured around."

Calena's mother was adamant about me getting in the front seat and wasn't taking no for an answer as she replied, *"I'm nobody's chauffeur so come up here in the front sweetie."*

I looked at her with this innocent look on my face as I slid from out of the back door to get into the front seat. I then closed the car door and put my seatbelt on before she started driving towards the Flea Market. As she promised, she let me pick my favorite color nail polish. It was very hot that day so we drove around with the windows down. On our way back, she got into the left turning lane as she came up to a four-way light, but we didn't have a clear turn until the light turned yellow. When the light turned from green to yellow, the other cars slowed down then she proceeded to make a left turn but a drunk driver kept driving. He hit the right side of the car where I would've been sitting if I didn't move when she told me. It happened so fast that our bodies jerked side-to-side from the impact of the accident; we were not expecting this on our way back to where I lived. It was a blessing that no one had any severe damages. When the ambulance arrived to the scene, they asked if I needed to go to the hospital. I was so shaken up that all I wanted to do was go home. My mother came up with my brother, Aunt Caroline and Calena to see if we were hurt. All I remember was being asked a million and one questions by them that I didn't want to answer. Later, Calena departed from us and went with her mother to the hospital in the ambulance truck. After that day, it was hard to get me to ride with anyone other than my mother.

A couple of weeks passed after the car accident, and going into the seventh grade without Commelina was the weirdest feeling ever. Without my crutches, it seemed like all hell broke loose; even though I wasn't limping physically, I was mentally. I tried to befriend other young girls, but it wasn't the same. It just seemed like matters grew worse; the girls I called myself being around picked fights with other girls and stayed in trouble all the time. I remember getting into a fight for passing a math test. When this tall girl stepped to my desk, I tried everything in my power to prevent us from fighting.

She looked down at me saying, "You think you smarter than me because you got a B on the test?"

I respond with a dumbfounded look on my face saying, "I don't want to fight you."

She knew I didn't want to fight her, but it didn't stop her from punching me in the face.

Seconds later, it registered, and I slammed her to the ground, hoping that would calm her down. She was full of anger while one of the boys held her down until the school security came to take us both to the office. I couldn't believe that I was fighting for getting a good grade on my math test. I ended up getting suspended from school for two days.

After going through that, I started hanging around a relative, but she made enemies quickly for calling some girls baldheaded. By being around her consistently, they assumed I said the same thing about them so they wanted to jump me too. The truth is that they were called baldheaded, just not by me.

In middle school, we had seven different classes. During block changing one day, I was walking in the hallway to my next class. Approximately ten girls were behind me a couple of feet back, threatening to beat me up. My bottled emotions wanted to be released by grabbing one of the girls from the group and fighting her until I saw blood, but word traveled back to one of my eighth-grade friends. Before I could turn around, a couple of eighth graders came in between us. One of the eight graders said, "Ya'll got to fight us first!" The seven grade girls saw it was more girls than them, which scared the girls away.

Experiencing these different conflicts made me hate going to school. I dreaded getting up to go to that place. I just wanted to go far away and never return. Luckily, I talked to Commelina every day; she heard sad story after sad story from me, and if we talked about anything good, it was when she talked about going to her new school and meeting new friends. As much as she enjoyed being in Atlanta, GA, she said it was nothing like home.

I realized staying out of trouble was going to take changing my circle of friends and hanging around mature eighth graders. It prevented me from getting into trouble with the other seventh graders who disliked me because they thought I sat around and talked about them. At this point, going through different situations in middle school and the car accident made me feel as if I didn't need to be alive. In fact, if the girls had known what I really had gone through or the suicidal thoughts on my mind, they probably would have thought twice about mistreating me. Just maybe they would have left me alone and found someone else to target.

My eighth-grade year went a little smoother. Commelina returned after living with her dad for about a year. She met my brother before he went back to Lake City, Florida. She and my other girl friends had the biggest crush on my brother after they saw him walk around the house with his boxers on. When he moved, all she talked about was how fine my brother looked walking in the kitchen with his boxers. She noticed how protective I was over our friendship, but not to the point of being too clingy.

Commelina saw a change in me that semester. She saw how I embraced other students she called her friends. I was a little more open and vibrant. I made the honor roll so that I could run for eighth grade prom queen. I proved to myself that year that I could do anything I set my mind to. Before, I was the type of student who did enough to get by. Well let me tell you, I pushed myself and won Junior High Prom

Queen and made all A's and one B. Growing up, my mother had to work two jobs, so I really didn't have that extra help like most children. I had to learn a lot on my own by watching what I was exposed to. I had to overcome my deepest fears and depression. I can honestly say that I did for the time being.

I learned to stand on my own without depending on Commelina, my crutch. If I wanted to face this world, I had to experience what it was like surviving basic issues that came my way. It was good that Commelina left my life for that period of time so that I could be stronger independently. I needed that strength going into high school to experience that I was capable of becoming someone great. In that three-year time frame, l learned one simple thing about myself: I could walk on my own without using crutches.

"Keeping bad energy around is like walking into a trap. You didn't see it coming until you felt the pain from it."

--Shupier Jones

6

PRESSURE ISN'T ALWAYS BAD

Many times, we go through life not knowing our purpose or God given gift. Most people believe in doing what they've seen, been taught, or told to do when deciding which path they should take. Have you ever asked these questions? "Who am I? What is my purpose? Why am I only good at doing some things but other things I'm not? What is my God given talent? Why am I good at multiple things? Why do I have a talent I don't like to use?" If you asked yourself more than one of these questions, then we have something in common. I asked myself those questions when I started High School. For that very reason, I tell people all the time that the worse thing a person can do is live life and not know his or her purpose. I truly believe you have some type of calling, whether it's good or bad. It's very important that you find what it is you're called to do and stick with it. After reading, you may be asking, "Where do I begin?" The truth is there are multiple ways to answer that question, but the prefect one is, "Start seeking the Most High." It's Him that orders your foot steps and will direct your walk in this journey called life.

It's amazing how God will manifest Himself in your life and show you that, without a shadow of a doubt, it was Him all along. You will be left feeling like you can't continue living life without really knowing your creator or His divine will for your life. He causes you to reflect on past situations you encountered over the years to help you better understand why you went through different experiences in your life. In other words, you will learn that nothing happens just by accident; there is a reason you went through trials and tribulations and that reason is to build your character out of them. It's very important to know about the inner light inside of you, a light that must shine to encourage others to walk in spirit and in truth.

It's sad that it takes most of us going through a bad situation to see that the Most High exists. I'm guilty of this very same thing and went through some dark moments many times to finally understand that there is a higher power. I was left speechless, full of questions and started self-evaluating. Believe it or not, the Most High started pulling on me at a young age. Believe me when I say that some of you reading this book have a calling on your life and don't even know it. Don't think it's coincidental that you're experiencing hardships time after time.

When you are chosen by the Most High, you'll go through this thing called pressure. Pressure is life lessons that feel uneasy, but in actuality, they're designed to turn you into something beautiful. Also, it's not a setback to experience some negative forces. It's like you are a pearl made of dirt that gets trapped inside of a shell. The pearl goes through pressure before it becomes a beautiful pearl. Just like it doesn't make sense that dirt turns into a pearl from being inside of a shell, sometimes, the very thing that doesn't make sense ends up being the very thing that brings light to your dark situation. The dirty moments I had in life caused me to experience a lot of pressure.

In this chapter, I discuss how being under pressure helped me discover that a true living God has a purpose for my existence.

Dirty girl, come as you are...

I started high school on September 8, 1997. I went to a school that was fairly new, so literally, we were the first graduating class who attended all four years. I knew very few students because it was an academy school that choose students from all over Dade County through the lottery or tryouts. A mixture of students came from the North and South to attend one of the best schools ever built in Miami. I had very few friends; I mainly hung around my cousin and the students who rode the bus from my neighborhood. I entered in the Business and Finance program, but I really wanted to be in the Performing Arts Academy. Those students seemed to have the most fun. For that very reason, I made sure that most of my electives were based around acting and music. When my drama teacher saw my potential, she hated that I wasn't picked for performing arts; she felt that I was destined to be a great actress and script writer.

I met Hazel in drama class, who ended up becoming one of my closest friends. I was drawn to her because every time class was in session, she would rest her head on top of a thick book. Some days, she read the book instead of being active with the rest of the class. I noticed her stomach started getting bigger and that she stayed asleep half of the time. I became more and more curious with what Hazel had going on, especially the book she carried around.

It was the beginning of the school year, so I carried my black bag around a lot for basketball season. I remember walking into class and seeing an empty desk next to Hazel. I sat down at the desk and placed my black bag on the floor. I looked her way and tapped her on the shoulder. When she stood up, she looked around and noticed I was the only one who could have tapped her on the back of her shoulder.

I asked her the first thing that came to mind, "What's the name of the book you're reading?"

She replied, "What book?"

I said, "*The book you always sleeping on!*"

"*You talking about this Amplified Bible,*" said Hazel.

"*Yeah,*" I responded.

Then, I asked her, "*What is an Amplified Bible?*"

"*It's a study Bible that helps you understand the Bible better; it's written in story form,*" said Hazel.

"*I really don't study the Bible like that but can you teach me?*" I asked.

She said, "*Yes, I can do the best I can!*"

Hazel didn't know that teaching me about our Creator changed my life forever. She introduced me to the very thing I was missing in my life: the living word of GOD. I would be lying if I said my life changed overnight because it didn't. All I can say is that a seed was planted, a seed that will one day manifest as a deeply rooted tree that's not easily moved. I learned a lot through Hazel about my Creator, Christ and the Holy Spirit. I hated that she had to stop coming to school. Later, I found out that Hazel's stomach was getting bigger because she was pregnant. She had to transfer to another school created for teen mothers for safety and to continue their education. I kept reading about Christ and other chosen people in the Bible; however, my focus was on playing basketball on a college level.

I made captain and a name for myself on the basketball court from my freshmen year all the way to my senior year. Basketball season was my favorite time of the year for one simple reason...support. Even though my mother and I didn't have the best mother and daughter relationship, she made sure to be at the majority of my home and away games. Every now and then, my best friend Commelina came to my games with her boyfriend Black, who later became the father of her children. My father may have come to one or two of my games. If you want to know the truth, I really didn't expect for him to show up since he really wasn't active in my life.

On August 16, 1999, I started my first job working at OfficeMax as a cashier. I was under a lot of pressure since I was a full-time student, working and playing sports, such as basketball and running track. My mother wanted me to be independent, but she demonstrated it in a controlling way by taking the checks I made and giving me only a certain amount each pay period. We bumped heads a lot because I didn't understand that she was preparing me to save for what was yet to come, like a rainy day. I wanted all of my money to keep up with the latest trends, like the other students at school. Those who wore the name brand shoes and clothes were more prone to fit in with the more popular students. At school, popularity was based more on materialistic things and how well you played a sport than academics. I was blinded; looking to be validated by my peers instead of realizing validation comes from the Most High. I should've known when I was drawn to Hazel's bible. If I paid attention then, I wouldn't have started walking in the wrong direction, but I did. I stopped connecting with what gave me strength. I was caught up in pleasing self needs when my focus should have been on pleasing the Most High. Since I didn't do that, all hell broke loose and the pressure unfolded.

One of my very first pressure experiences began when I was part of a female click in High School. For some reason, I ended up being the one they lashed out on over the stupidest things. In most cases, it was over a boy, the clothes I wore or a person they didn't like that they saw me talking to. It got so bad that I had two girls come to my job trying to pick a fight with me over a boy. Both managers held me back while they escorted both girls out the store. I almost lost my job for acting unseemly in the work place. Although I was provoked that experience was a wakeup call for me; I became mature very fast. I am happy that I maintained my behavior on my job from that day. My mother got me a brand-new car a couple of months later, right after I received my driver's license. Having good behavior wasn't the only reason my mother bought me a new car; really, it had to do with her getting tired of driving me everywhere.

Having a car wasn't a good thing for me at all. By my junior year, I went to many places I had no business going. I went up north to the city to meet young thug boys, I went to parties that turned into shootouts, I snuck into clubs with friends knowing we were under age, I stole clothes with my friends out of the mall, I skipped school, I hung out at the ghetto flea markets, I got into a minor car accident by driving to close and I movie hopped to catch up on all the latest films. My conscience ate at me from time-to-time, but it did not stop me from doing what I wanted to do. I was one of the fortunate ones who didn't get caught in my wrong doing until grace and mercy took a vacation and left me in the company of harm's way.

I stepped out of my league into a world I wasn't mentally equipped for at my age. I had unprotected sex with my first partner and ended up getting a STD (sexually transmitted disease). I was in love with an experienced guy who loved to date strippers. It took me three days to tell my mother about an uncomfortable feeling in my vagina. Not only did it hurt to lose my virginity, it also itched like hell. I was completely unaware of the precautions to take when sexually active. I thought I knew it all, but the Creator taught me a valuable lesson at a young age about sex; it's nothing to play around with if you're not consciously aware of its true meaning. I was fortunate to also learn it was something curable, but the embarrassing feeling stayed because my mother had to find out her daughter was no longer a virgin. That's when pressure revealed itself again; I felt dirty, betrayed and alone. Then, I heard Hazel's voice in my head saying, "When I'm in trouble, I just read the Bible." Instantly, I decided to change one thing about myself; I found one of my mother's old Bible and started reading it more. I found life reading the Bible and learned the Creator uses the poor, less likely, weirdest looking, uneducated and most disliked person for His glory. The saddest part is that I knew the

Creator wanted me to learn something out of this situation, but as soon as I was healed, I went back to being disobedient.

"Life is understood better when you look at it backwards. You learn that your mistakes were lessons to prepare you for your purpose."

--Shupier Jones

7

OBEDIENCE IS BETTER THAN SACRIFICE

Every wrong thing you do doesn't always send karma your way. However, when you're consciously aware of your actions, karma knocks at your front door unexpectedly. Most people believe karma is a sign of payback for the wrong doing done in the past. You may have recalled having this experience before; at the same time, you probably weren't expecting that certain thing to happen and repay you with vengeance. When it happens, you realize that your pay didn't come in the form of money because you were paid back with suffering and regret. Furthermore, I believe karma has a mind of its own and makes special appearances when you least expect it. I think it happens to show you it's time to change those bad habits of yours.

Most of us know that a visit from karma is usually a sign of payback for hurting someone intentionally. The scary part is that you didn't know the type of gift karma would bring you; as a matter of fact, I know it's not designed to be a pleasurable moment. Given your name is engraved on a package that is specially wrapped for you, it tends to be something you don't want because it leaves you feeling in a dark state of mind and worse than the hurt you caused. Consequently, the gift inside is payback for the pain you did towards a specific person. Also, karma reminds you of the cause of the visit-- a wrong decision you made that revealed the iniquity in your heart.

Imagine having that same type of behavior towards the Creator. In fact, this is one of the biggest mistakes you can easily make when you become a lover of yourself and do what you want when you want to. Being a lover of yourself happens when you begin following your will instead of being led by the will of the

Most High. You become that person who's careless and inconsiderate of others. For instance, you're intrigued with your knowledge instead of seeking wisdom, knowledge and understanding from the very GOD who created us all. I feel karma brings about punishment for these two reasons: first, to set the tone so that you can fulfill your divine purpose on Earth and second, to give you multiple testimonies to share with unbelievers who have strayed from the light, the way, and the truth.

I remember a time that karma brought me a first-class fight to death and the devil. Luckily, I had a delay that helped me get back on the right track. I learned through different experiences that the Most High God warns you before destruction. He gives you time to get it right and change your wicked ways by putting you in situations that cause you to self-reflect on your past behavior. He knew I needed something to happen to help me stay on the right path to help build His Kingdom. I had to go through some stumbling blocks to see the Creator's power at hand and change my view of life. He created a new heart in me and renewed my mind by placing me eyeball-to-eyeball with the Devil's advocate...karma. During this chapter of my life, I felt the shield of protection lifting, allowing me to be attacked by the enemy. At that moment, my feelings, thoughts and experiences helped me to understand that this life of mine is bigger than me, and the purpose for my existence is much greater than what I could possibly imagine.

A life-threatening situation bridged the gap between the Most High and me spiritually. Although I came across a lot of stumbling blocks that felt like setbacks, they actually were used to detour me from heading down the path of destruction.

It's not by accident this happened

My last year in high school was the most stressful year ever. Between senior activities, working, playing basketball and having a college boyfriend, I had no free-time. Honestly, the hardest thing for me was when I finally started a committed relationship with Anthony.

I met Anthony, during a High School football game on a Friday night. I went with my cousin Pam to see her school play against their rivalry school. The stadium was filled with people from the south side of Miami. The only bleachers available were below a crowd of thuggish looking boys. My cousin knew a few of them but I kept my back facing them since I did know them. Suddenly, I get a push on my back. Seconds later, I turned around and all I remember seeing were guys with dread locks with a mouth full of gold teeth. I was scared but I didn't show it. I looked at all of them but no one spoke a word. Instantly, I became mad and caught an attitude.

> I felt weird and uncomfortable so I told my cousin, *"Hey, I want to go sit on the other side. Someone just push me on my back and nobody ain't saying nothing."*

She said, "Okay!"

Before I knew it, Anthony made his way towards the other side where we were and told a girl sitting above us to hook him up with me. She waited until Anthony walked off before delivering the message. By then, Anthony was waiting by the fence for me to come. My cousin Pam vouched for him immediately and informed me that he's a good dude. I looked at them both and remembered feeling very nervous. My cousin pushed me and told me to go talk to him. I turned my head to look his way and started walking towards him. We talked the last quarter of the game. It was history after that because he later became my first college boyfriend.

Growing up in Miami as a female, it was common to date a guy with dreadlocks and gold teeth, in other words, a thug. Anthony fit that description very well; he just had a little more going for himself, like playing football on a college level. Having a long-distance relationship with Anthony was healthier for me when he was away. I can testify that staying loyal to Anthony kept me out of trouble and away from being sexually active with guys who tried hard to get my attention.

When Anthony came home, I felt like I was in the relationship by myself; our time was limited with one another because he focused more on his friends and other females. Besides, he said repeatedly, *"I'm not ready for a girlfriend."* Of course, I didn't listen. It was like my mother saying that I couldn't drive a car she bought for me. If we did spend time, it was mainly watching him play videos games and smoking weed with his homeboys inside his room. The only quality time we really had was taking our clothes off to have sex, but it only lasted a few minutes because we were always interrupted by his friend Earl, who stayed on his tail. I always felt suspicions about Earl because he stayed around us instead of being around his girlfriend. I truly believed he was an undercover brother due to him having too many feminine ways. Anthony had to argue with Earl for him to stay away from us for a couple of days. I loved when they disagreed because it gave Anthony and me more time with each other.

Anthony was the type who was loved by many and hated by few. So, often times, I felt like I was in competition with his friends. I was so busy trying to win his love that I lost myself in the midst of it. I put all my focus in loving him when I should have been focused on preparing for playing basketball on a college level. My close friends noticed something was wrong when my weight surprisingly started going up and down. It started when Anthony's behavior changed towards me. I knew when he ignored me that he was cheating with other girls. I lost my appetite from being depressed, which caused my weight to fluctuate. I remember feeling suicidal, unloved and depressed all the time. I started slacking in school, on my job and in basketball. Anthony had total control, and I gave him permission to have it. I was so in love with Anthony that I didn't realize I wasn't loving myself.

> When the holiday break was over, Anthony had to return to college. His mother and I grew a close bond. She was the one who talked me into staying in a relationship with her son. She would always tell me, "Baby, he will come around one day. Ever since his grand-mother passed away, he's been afraid to love. You're good for him. He just can't see it right now."

Anthony's mom knew my patience was running thin when I would respond, *"Yes, ma'am. I just hope he doesn't wait too late."*

I made sure to visit his mother a couple of days of the week since she didn't have transportation. I took her places when she needed to handle personal business or had doctor's appointments. The type of relationship we had was like a mother and daughter who shared a close bond. She treated me like the daughter she never had. Spending a lot of time with her made me feel obligated to make sure she was well taken care of while her son was off to college. I was too young and naive to see the load of burdens I carried. I walked away from the things that would eventually make me a better person to help someone who wasn't in the position to better me mentally and physically. I put my boyfriend and his family before my personal needs and slowly started to drift away from the path created for me. I left from walking on a lighted path to a path that was dark and gloomy.

At this point, I gave up on things I loved or had hopes of becoming. It seemed like the more I stayed around Anthony and his family, the more I consumed the habits, behaviors and mentality of his family. No matter how hard I screamed inside for help, it was hard for any soul to hear me. My close friends tried to make sense of my relationship with Anthony. They knew deep down that something was wrong with my dating life when my tears threw me under the bus. However, there wasn't too much convincing they could have done since I stayed in the relationship. My problem was I thought I could change Anthony's feelings to love me the way I loved him. I should have invested that time and money back into me, but I was weak-minded. I was busy looking for love in all the wrong places. Instead of focusing and trusting the Creator, I put my focus and trust in a boy. HE warned me on several occasions to obey Him; instead of listening, I did what I wanted to do; doing what I wanted sent karma my way.

God sent me an Angel

On school days, I set my clock for 6:00am to make it to school on time. Majority of the time, I was late from being in the shower too long, so half of the time, I rushed out the house to get in my car and drive off to school. On my way to school one day, I had no idea that I was about to experience a visit from karma. I drove the same route to school every morning unless one of my friends called for me to pick them up for school. As I was coming out of my neighborhood, I made a left turn onto a main street. When I got to the end of the road, I made another left turn to drive to a main highway.

That morning, the weather was a little misty, but the sun was rising and the traffic was pretty normal like any other morning. Before approaching the silver car ahead of me, I used my left hand to push down the black handle to turn on the left signal to move around a Lincoln town car. I looked to my left side to see if it was safe to move over into the left lane. When it was clear, I moved over and noticed a white pickup truck ahead of me in the left lane too. Seconds later, I looked in my right rear-view mirror and saw a sea green Honda speeding in the right lane. I glanced quickly over to my right side while the driver sped past me. All of a sudden, the driver in the sea green Honda cut over in the left lane and slammed on the brakes to make a left-hand turn. Quickly, the driver in the white pickup truck pressed on his brakes. When I slammed on my brakes, my life flashed right before my eyes while trying to prevent hitting the white truck in the rear.

Apparently, I didn't press down fast enough because the airbag came towards me in slow motion as my car went under his truck. I was blessed that when my car went under the truck, it pushed the truck forward and my car to the right side of the road out of ongoing traffic. Smoke started coming from under the hood of the car; then the car driver's door opened. I felt dizzy getting out the door after the car accident. Quickly, a flashback of my very first car accident came to mind, and I felt all those same emotions again. I couldn't believe I was involved in an accident twice on the same street but on the opposite side of the street.

I snapped out of it when a Hispanic woman with short dark hair who looked to be in her mid-thirties grabbed me by the arm and caught me before I fell to the ground.

> She said, "Sweetie, are you alright? I've called 911; they are on their way."

"I'm okay," I said.

> She took her phone from her packet and asked, "What's your mom's number?"

I dialed the number for her and looked at her with tears flowing down my face in total shock. She stayed with me the whole time until the police came to the scene. When we heard sirens, the police and ambulance had to be near. The officer hurried and parked his car then came over to where we were sitting. He asked that I step to the side to answer some questions. We walked to the side of the police car to get my side of the story; as we conversed, he wrote in a small, black notebook. After we finished, the officer escorted me to get checked by the paramedics.

I sat down in the ambulance for them to see if I needed to go to the hospital. I told them that I refused to go the hospital and that I was fine. My mother finally made it to the scene when she received the call saying that her daughter had just been in a car accident. She placed her hand over her mouth and looked at me as if she'd seen a ghost standing in front of her. Once I was finished getting checked on, I told my mother to take me to school. I stared at my car and saw the damage that blew my mind away. The front part of the car ended up being pushed back to the windshield. The thought of the accident replaying over and over in my mind was depressing, and staying in the house alone would make matters worse. I just wanted to go to school and be around friends who could help me get through this life changing time.

"Are you sure you want to go to school?" my mother asked.

"Yes, momma. I am sure." I replied.

I looked around for the Hispanic lady who helped me get out of the car, but she was nowhere to be found. I walked around to ask the officer and the paramedic if they had seen a Hispanic lady with short black hair, but they all shook their head back and forth saying, "No." I looked around one last time as I got into my mother's car to head off to school. Feeling lost and confused about what happened, I stared out the window and started thinking about the lady who helped me out of the car. I felt like she was some type of guardian angel because I later found out that all the doors were jammed, so it would've been impossible for me to get out of the car on my own. I also thought that day could have been my last, so it was time for me to get my act together.

Thankful to see another birthday

My mother rented a car for me to get back and forth to school while my car was getting fixed at the auto shop. I laid low and stayed to myself after the car accident to get my thoughts together. It was something jarring about a life changing experience happening during my teenage years. If being in that car accident didn't get my attention, then I didn't know what else would have. I could have been dead and gone, but the message from karma opened my eyes quickly. In my spare time, I wrote poems of things I was feeling; then, I changed them into lyrics. I realized I could express my pain in music. The song, "Lord Knows" was my first song. It reminded me that no matter how hard I tried, I could not do it by myself. I realized that the Creator will get your attention, especially when you are disobedient to the calling designed for you.

On my 18th birthday (December 14, 2000), I reflected on all the things I encountered over the years and thought about how I survived them all. My mother threw me a big birthday party. When it was time for me to blow out the candles, I understood that I couldn't continue to mistreat the very one who created me. Although I knew I was imperfect, there was a greater calling for my life. I realized that my decisions would determine whether I fulfilled my purpose on this Earth.

My high school years were a big eye opener. I learned that obedience is better than sacrifice. Regardless of how many chances you think you are getting away with, you will never supersede the punishment. When you think you have more time, your time gets cut short. I had to tell myself that I wasn't put on Earth just to do what I wanted to do; I was placed to be used as a tool to save the lost souls. I had to experience and feel what it was like being a lost soul, being broken. In fact, you can't preach or teach unless you've been through the storm and studied who the Creator really is.

Over the years, life taught me a few things. If I had to redo anything over again, I would not because the best teacher has been my experiences, thoughts and feelings. I can rewind, replay and relive each past memory to remind myself of one thing: I am going to conquer and defeat the inner demon.

This is why the Creator isn't done with me yet; this is just the beginning of me putting it all on paper!

ABOUT THE AUTHOR

Known as an actress and model that has appeared on the Lifetime Network, Black Entertainment Television (BET) and in Hotlanta Magazine, Shupier Jones wants to be best known as a woman determined to help women face their untold stories of shame, hurt and regret. As a professional hairstylist of more than 20 years, Shupier not only has been positioned to hear the countless stories of women broken by painful experiences but has committed to assisting others in working through the haunting fear and unforgettable pain of their past. Shupier understands this fear because it took her years to deal with the resentment, anxiety and anger she developed as a result of being molested as a child. Though an accomplished actress, model and hairstylist, Shupier secretly carried many painful memories throughout her life. True to the meaning of her name "Dependable upon God," Shupier needed God to move beyond her past.

As a mother desiring to protect her two beautiful, precious daughters and a woman wanting to please the Most High in all things,

Shupier decided it was time to face her painful past by *Putting It All On Paper*, which is the title of her memoir that recounts the painful memories that held Shupier in bondage. More importantly, the memoir recounts the healing process Shupier allowed the Most High to guide her through to become better, stronger and more committed to helping others. *Putting It All on Paper* has released Shupier from the shame and hate she carried for years and freed her to willingly share her past and love the people who hurt her. As a speaker, Shupier desires for other people, especially women, to be free of negative feelings and obsession with what others think about them. She wants people to let go of their negative past so that it doesn't affect their relationships, health, self-esteem and future. She wants to encourage others to live their best lives.

NOW IT'S YOUR TURN

*Write your story...*_____

PUTTING IT ALL ON PAPER

www.ingramcontent.com/pod-product-compliance
Lightning Source LLC
Chambersburg PA
CBHW021127300426
44113CB00006B/313